"I picked up your book out of cur~~iosity~~ ~~~~ ~~~~
it straight through. Thank you for writing it!"

—EUGENE PETERSON, translator of *The Message*

"Here is a book that needs to be read. It's interesting, relevant, and extremely important."

—GEORGE VERWER, founder and president of
Operation Mobilisation, author of *Out of the Comfort Zone*

"Sam Williamson draws on his personal experience and evangelical heritage to offer a book rich with practical wisdom that can help Christians of all traditions learn to hear God in their lives."

—RALPH MARTIN, host of *The Choices We Face*

"A key longing in every human heart is to connect with God, to actually hear his voice. Sam Williamson has written a remarkable book that teaches both how to hear God's voice in Scripture, and then to hear his voice in every avenue of life. It's filled with humor, insight, practical tips, and sound theology. I can't recommend a better guide than *Hearing God in Conversation*."

—GARY WILKERSON, pastor, president of World Challenge

"In *Hearing God in Conversation*, Samuel Williamson affirms the church's long-held position that God's primary means of speaking to us is through Scripture; at the same time, through a blend of Bible teaching, contemporary and classic Christian authors, and personal experience, he shows us that God is in no way limited in terms of what he can use to prompt us, nudge us, and lead us. Written in a casual, sometimes light-hearted style, *Hearing God in Conversation* propels us to a place of expectancy with respect to God's voice; to look for God's personal message to us in a variety of circumstances; and to be aware that God has a vast array of means he uses to guide his children."

—PAUL WILKINSON, former writer for Christianity Today's
Leadership Journal

"If you want to grow in your ability to recognize how God makes himself known to you, I can't recommend a better guide than Samuel Williamson's *Hearing God in Conversation*. This is not the advice of an expert who has it all figured out, but the humility of a brother still on the journey who recognizes that at best we see in bits and pieces. But that is enough to mark out an amazing adventure with God. You will find the stories from his own life engaging, insightful, and helpful."

—WAYNE JACOBSEN, pastor, author of *He Loves Me*

"This book is a rare gem, full of spiritual wisdom, practical insight, and personal examples of how God converses with us in our daily lives. I was captivated from the first page to the last. Sam Williamson is a great natural storyteller, a sound biblical narrator and armchair theologian, and a wise counselor with spiritual depth and insight.

"He is also an excellent writer—easy to read and joyful to follow. Reading his book is like carrying on an enlightening conversation with an experienced and faith-filled friend while sitting in an easy chair enjoying one another's company. You can't savor enough and you want to come back for more and more.

"The book is balanced in dealing with potential pitfalls and aberrations. It treats the need for discernment, how to distinguish God's voice from other voices, how filters and biases can shape and block our ability to hear God's voice, and the role of community in helping us discern and confirm God's word for us."

—DON SCHWAGER, author of DailyScripture.net

"'God is always speaking to us, and he wants us to hear him.' In *Hearing God in Conversation* Sam Williamson gives us some tools to do just that. He does a masterful job in leading us to this end with honesty, insight, and great advice. He writes about deep things with clarity and a disarming humor, helping the reader to explore new territory in hearing God's voice."

—DAVID MANGAN, author of *God Loves You and There's Nothing You Can Do About It*

"Hearing God. Is it real? Is it normal? Is it weird? Sam grew up in a Christian family where listening to God was as normal and frequent as conversing with family members around the dinner table. It was simply what a relationship with God looked like for everyone, everyplace, all the time. Sam has done a brilliant job explaining, through Scripture, stories, and personal experiences, how God speaks and how to hear him."

—GARY BARKALOW, author, founder of The Noble Heart

Hearing *God* in Conversation

Also by the Author
Is Sunday School Destroying Our Kids?

Hearing *God* in Conversation

HOW TO RECOGNIZE HIS VOICE EVERYWHERE

Samuel C. Williamson

FOREWORD BY PAUL E. MILLER

Kregel
Publications

ISBN 978-0-8254-4424-1

Printed in the United States of America
16 17 18 19 20 21 22 23 24 25 / 5 4 3 2 1

I dedicate this book to my father,
Robert Samuel Williamson,
who taught me how to hear God's voice in Scripture,
to walk with him in the cool of the day,
and to talk with him on my drive to work.
He now walks with his heavenly Father,
face-to-face.

Contents

Foreword

When it comes to listening to God, most of us get nervous. We love the idea of tuning in to our Father's voice, especially amid the constant noise of our own lives and hearts, or the constant input from the world around us. C. S. Lewis aptly called our culture "the Kingdom of Noise." But the idea of hearing the Father's voice as it applies to the details of our lives scares us. We don't trust what we are hearing or thinking because we have seen people overspiritualize their emotional responses. Yet we don't want to live as functional atheists, either. It is a valid concern.

But the desire to hear God does not go away. Deep down we want to develop an eye for the One who has promised to lead us with his voice. Imagine a road with two deep ditches that constantly threaten to disable us. On the one side, there is the ditch of post-Enlightenment rationalism. On the other is the ditch of highly subjective emotionalism. If we travel a little too close to either side, we tumble down into the ditch. No wonder we get frustrated.

Unfortunately, such frustration can lead to a shutting down of the heart. Unbelief that God really cares about the nitty-gritty details of one's life begins to take over. Before we know it, all that is left is unbelief, and we stop praying altogether. A quiet defeat takes over. Prayerlessness wins the day. It feels like God is a million miles away and that even he doesn't realize it. It's easy to conclude that he is asking way too much of us.

Besides giving in to a quiet prayerlessness, what does such defeat look like? It is easy to look at the "Word only" approach to listening to God. Carefully and prudently, we seek passages of Scripture—any passages—that can shed light on our situation. We cry out for help but, deep down, we are bothered because it can seem that Scripture only applies to people in general. God's Word can seem too abstract at times to really help us. Our Father, the Shepherd, is only paying lip service. He does not mean it when he says for me to "ask, seek, wait, obey" and watch what happens.

We have become deists, having successfully removed an intimately interested God from our lives.

Christians can be just as stuck in the opposite ditch. Instead of "Word only," we make too much of our emotions. This is the elevation of one's own intuition to the status of divine revelation. We decide to take control, and our emotions, at the expense of the Word, win the day. We become subjective. We become goofy. It is embarrassing.

Just what is the solution to getting stuck by rationalism on the one hand or emotionalism on the other?

The call in our lives to guard against rationalism and emotionalism drives us to seek God in the sharp-edged, absolute character of the Word and the intuitive, personal leading of the Spirit. The Word gives us the structure—the vocabulary, if you will—while the Spirit personalizes it to our life. Keeping the Word and the Spirit together guards us from God-talk becoming a cover for our own desires or from living isolated from God.

The book you hold in your hands is just such much-needed help. I am delighted that Sam Williamson has given us such a great gift. In it, to use Sam's words, he heads straight into "hearing God beyond the lectures," and he does so with disarming honesty about his own frustrations, carefully thinking through Scripture while laying out the necessary balance between the Word and the Spirit.

Your Father wants you to be praying. He wants you asking. He wants you inviting him into the details of your life. Sam gives help in the pages ahead. He will help us get out of the ditch and back onto the road of richer, deeper relationship with the Father. It all begins with hearing God.

—PAUL E. MILLER
Author of *A Praying Life: Connecting with God in a Distracting World*,
and *A Loving Life: In a World of Broken Relationships*

My Parents' Gift of Extraordinary Ordinariness

*There is not in the world a kind of life more sweet and delightful
than that of a continual conversation with God. Those only can
comprehend it who practice and experience it. . . . Let us do it
from a principle of love, and because God would have us.*
—Brother Lawrence

*[When Adam and Eve] heard the sound of the Lord God walking
in the garden in the cool of the day, [they] hid themselves from
the presence of the Lord God among the trees of the garden.*
—Genesis 3:8

The family culture that nurtures us in our youth also cultivates in us a sense of ordinariness, perhaps even diminishment, concerning that upbringing: *What's the big deal? Doesn't everyone think this way?* My wife's family were sports fanatics. She was shocked to discover I had not once watched the annual Thanksgiving Day football game. *Doesn't everyone?*

My parents taught us kids how to hear God. I simply assumed that everyone expected to hear God's voice in their lives. I once shared with a small group of men my story of the first time God spoke to me as a ten-year-old. One of the men pulled me aside and forcefully suggested that

I never share the story again. He said no one would believe it happened to such a young kid.

Yet when he himself was ten, this man knew every name of every starting player on every NBA basketball team. I never would have believed it. Until I met my wife's brothers.

My parents practiced family devotions on us reluctant children. Every evening after dinner they taught worship, Bible study, intercession, and hearing God; they revealed to us the *meaning* of a divine relationship. They shared stories of God speaking to them, and we read books about Christians called by God. My parents even conducted practical labs with us: how to see God in Scripture, how to brainstorm with God, and how to hear his voice when praying for each other.

To me, it just seemed so ordinary, the way that the Christian life is meant to be walked. I've found, however, that hearing God is anything but normal for many believers. What my parents taught as ordinary is usually considered extraordinary.

But it's meant to be ordinary.

My parents taught us that we were redeemed in order to have a restored relationship with God. And the basis of every real relationship is communication; God saved us to have a conversational relationship with him. The temple curtain was torn in two so that we can connect with him again.

He calls to us, "Walk with me."

Why Does God Save Us?

In 2006, *Christianity Today*'s managing editor published a list of the twentieth century's top fifty books that shaped the evangelical world.[1] His number one influential book was not written by C. S. Lewis, John Stott, or Dietrich Bonhoeffer. It wasn't even Kenneth Taylor's *The Living Bible* (which was number six).

The number one book was written by an author few of us have heard of, and yet it has influenced every single one of us. This book was written by Rosalind Rinker, and it was titled *Prayer: Conversing with God*. She introduced the Christian world to praying with conversational language. No more *Thees*, *Thous*, and *which-arts*. Just everyday language.

She revolutionized our modern prayer life with the simple declaration, "Prayer is a dialogue between two persons who love each other."[2]

Ask believers what distinguishes Christianity from other religions and many will answer, "Other religions are works-based; in Christianity we are saved by grace. Buddha's last words were, 'Strive without ceasing,'[3] but Christ's last words were, 'It is finished.'"[4] At immeasurable cost—the cost of the cross—God himself entered into history and acted to save us.

But save us for what?

God saved us for more than good behavior and right thinking—for more, not less. The triune God, in whose image we are made, saved us to restore us to a relationship with himself.

In the garden of Eden, God once talked with Adam and Eve in the cool of the day in a conversational relationship with his beloved creatures. Then, through humanity's disobedience, a barrier of unrighteousness formed, and our relationship with God was broken.

But God loved his creation—"For God so loved the world"—and he formed a plan to heal that relational breach. In that plan, Jesus saved us *away from* our sinfulness and saved us *back into* that conversational relationship with him. On the cross, the cry of Jesus, "It is finished," also cries out to us, "Come walk with me."

Jesus called his disciples with this simple invitation, "Come, follow me." They immediately joined him on the road and began to walk with God. This is the call of God to every believer. Jesus invites us to walk with him. It is the invitation of a relational heart.

I Offer What I've Been Taught

In this book I share what I've learned about conversing with God. It may seem the height of arrogance for any person to attempt to teach the world how to hear God. All I can say is, *I'm passing on to others only what others have passed on to me.* My parents bequeathed to me real gold; I want to pass their extraordinary treasure on to others.

I only share what I've personally learned, practiced, and seen bear fruit. I can't share what I don't know. This book includes no chapters on visions or dreams; I don't get them, at least not the spiritual kind. But I *have* learned how to hear God in the conversations of ordinary life.

Prayer is not a one-way street with us shouting petitions to God, and Scripture is not a one-way street of God broadcasting his commands at us. *Both* prayer and Scripture involve *both* hearing and speaking. We are participants, not spectators; dancers on the floor, not observers at the tables; actors on the stage, not onlookers in the theater. We are involved in a divine dialogue.

The words of Scripture overflow with the images of a relational God. We limit the infinite God when we restrict the ways he wants to speak to us. I was taught to hear God's voice in Scripture, and I hope I can pass this on to you. I was also taught how to recognize that same voice when he speaks to me through friends, strangers, and in my drive time to work. I hope to pass that on to you as well.

> We limit the infinite God when we restrict the ways he wants to speak to us.

I Offer My Own Experiences

I write this book primarily to teach how to have a conversation with God. Prayer, this "dialogue between two persons who love each other," is close to God's heart. Many of us have low expectations for hearing God. Yet in a crisis, almost all of us look to him for direction. Our problem is that the clarity of his directional words depends on our ability to recognize his voice. And that is hard to learn in a crisis. If we want to hear God in the storm, let's first learn to hear his voice in the calm.

Only in the last chapter do I write about how to recognize God's voice for guidance. The rest of the chapters address hearing him in the many and diverse methods and manners he speaks to us in ordinary life.

Throughout the book I share examples from my firsthand experiences of hearing God. I often preface these stories with disclaimers such as, "I *thought* I heard God say . . ." However, since I don't begin each story with such a qualification, I will add that general disclaimer here: When I say in this book that I "heard" God, I only mean to say I *think* I heard him.

Though I really do believe I heard him!

Some Christians today believe that God no longer speaks outside of

Scripture. I disagree. There are excellent arguments for the belief that God speaks directly and personally today. But I don't want to cloud the chapters with arguments. Instead, I've included an appendix that summarizes the common arguments *against* and the common arguments *for* the belief that God speaks directly today. I call that appendix "Answers to the Arguments."

Other Christians are turned off by the odd, eccentric behavior of some "hearing" believers who practice immoderate, crazy customs that don't square with the rest of Scripture. I think we need to address those excesses as well. I speak to those behaviors in the second appendix, "Questionable and Excessive Practices."

To hear God, we need the help of his Holy Spirit. It is God himself, stirring his Spirit in us, who enables us to recognize his still, small voice. It is God calling to us and our hearts responding to him that forms the foundation of our conversational relationship. As C. S. Lewis wrote,

> They tell me, Lord, that when I seem
> To be in speech with you,
> Since but one voice is heard, it's all a dream,
> One talker aping two.
>
> Sometimes it is, yet not as they
> Conceive it. Rather, I
> Seek in myself the things I hoped to say,
> But lo! my wells are dry.
>
> Then, seeing me empty, you forsake
> The listener's role and through
> My dumb lips breathe and into utterance wake
> The thoughts I never knew.
>
> And thus you neither need reply
> Nor can; thus, while we seem
> Two talkers, thou art One forever, and I
> No dreamer, but thy dream.[5]

My hope is that we will all learn to hear the voice of God in conversation, his Spirit in ours, as we learn to walk with him.

—SAM
Ann Arbor, Michigan, May 2016

Acknowledgments

Our accomplishments in life often come at great cost to the ones we love most. We frequently forget their sacrifices and more frequently fail to acknowledge their gifts of time, listening, and care. I owe so much to so many. I cannot repay my debt to you, my friends and family, but let me at least acknowledge the lien you have on my life:

- My wife, Carla: I could never have written about hearing God without your sacrifice of listening to me, sometimes at the cost of my not listening to you. I love and thank you.
- My parents, Bob and Beulah: I barely grasp a hint of the fortune you bequeathed to me through your love, patience, and treasure trove of teaching.
- My son Jonathan: You spent scores of hours with me, poring over my manuscript, insisting on crispness, reminding me of the power of humor, and encouraging me to the finish line.
- The rest of my children and their spouses—Sam and Michele, David and Sarah, and Rebekah: You patiently endured hours of brainstorming and countless hours of listening to me read aloud my favorite sections.
- Gary Barkalow and John Hard, who encouraged me to detangle my thoughts through writing them down: You are my friends.
- Katherine McAulay: Though we've never met, your thoughtful reading helped shine light in the murky marshes of an incomplete manuscript.
- My editor, Bob Hartig: Your commitment to clean prose and your constant encouragement forged for me a new friendship.

Certain writers and speakers have influenced me so much that by now their thoughts have become my thoughts. I especially thank Oswald Chambers, C. S. Lewis, Dallas Willard, and Tim Keller, whose fingerprints are all over this book. Except on its weakest pages.

Chapter 1

The First Time I
Heard God's Voice

Why is it that when we speak to God we are said to be praying,
but when God speaks to us we are said to be schizophrenic?
—Lily Tomlin

I was ten years old the first time I heard God speak. It was autumn, a new school year had just begun, and a new fad was spreading among my adolescent classmates.

Cussing.

I was raised in a conservative Christian church where Sunday school teachers taught us the Ten Commandments. The teachers were vague about the meaning of adultery, and I didn't feel concerned. They weren't very clear about coveting either, so I felt safe.

They made up for their ambiguity when it came to cussing. Instead of an elusive "Don't take the name of the Lord in vain," they precisely taught, "Don't swear." And when they said, "Don't swear," they meant, "Don't cuss." For us, cussing was a sin on the order of mass genocide.

One day while playing school-yard tag, I tagged my girlfriend, Diane, and she shouted, "Shit!" I felt a horrible shock wave race through my body, as though I'd been hit in the gut with a sledgehammer. Forty-five years later, I still feel that visceral punch, and I can exactly picture the playground gate where Diane cussed. I gasped for air but nothing came.

Looking back, it seems silly that a cuss word could cause such a shock, but it did. I expected God to cast down a lightning bolt and burn Diane to ash. The thought almost paralyzed me.

Almost, but not quite. I leaped back seven feet in case the bolt went wide.

And then . . . nothing happened. Not one thing. The game continued. No lightning bolt. Not even a firefly. I felt as shocked by the absence of righteous retribution as I had been by the cuss. The shock might have even been greater.

My juvenile understanding of Christianity was simple: God blesses good people and he punishes bad people. In my unsophisticated ten-year-old mind, *blessing* meant being cool and *punishment* meant being uncool. But that's not what happened. Instead, the foul-mouthed kids became cooler while the clean-speaking kids grew uncool.

The wicked flourished and the righteous were trampled.

I decided that God could not exist. Oh, it took a week or so of watching the wicked prosper, but there was no doubt in my mind. God didn't exist. It was all a cruel hoax.

The next day I unleashed the filthiest mouth in the city of Detroit on my classmates. I said things even the wicked feared to say. (They still harbored some fear of God, but I knew better.) The sh-word was cussing for kids; I dropped f-bombs like hardwood forests drop autumn leaves—and I didn't even know what the f-word meant.

I was a poet in profanity.

Then, at the end of that day, alone in my bedroom, God spoke to me with a fierce, undeniable, and certain clarity. But all he said was, *"Sam, I am real, and you don't understand."*

God Wants Us to Know Him

Above all else, God wants us to know him personally—he wants a personal relationship. But we mostly want to know direction: "Should I take this job or that job?" We want information; God wants a conversation. We want to know answers; God wants us to know him.

When God spoke to me, I was deeply moved, but not by his answer to my question, why do the wicked flourish? God never even hinted at an answer. I was moved because I had actually heard his voice. I had begun to know the person of God, not just the facts of God; I had met him.

God always gives us what we most need, but he doesn't always give us what we *think* we most need. Our deepest need is to know God. More than answers, inspiration, information, or guidance, we simply need to know God. That's why Paul wrote, "I count everything as loss because of the surpassing worth of knowing Christ Jesus" (Phil. 3:8).

Before my first date with the woman who would become my wife, I knew a lot about her: she was a farmer's daughter, she studied social work, and she had attended Hope College. And she was cute. But on our first date, over a glass of wine, she told me of a secret longing. And I fell in love. My informational knowledge had just been trumped by a personal connection.

> God always gives us what we most need, but he doesn't always give us what we *think* we most need.

Knowing *about* God isn't enough. Paul prayed, "I keep asking that the God of our Lord Jesus Christ . . . may give you the Spirit of wisdom and revelation, *so that you may know him better*" (Eph. 1:16–17 SWP).

God Wants Us to Hear Him

God is always speaking to us, and he wants us to hear him. The first time I heard him in my bedroom—and I really did hear him—I wasn't looking to hear from God. I thought he was a hoax. But he spoke anyway, because he longs—God himself longs!—for conversations with his family and friends.

I am amazed, dumbfounded even, at modern Christian teaching. We hear leaders claim that Christianity is about a personal relationship with God, but their teaching is limited to abstract doctrine, principles for good behavior, or devotional inspiration. In other words, most modern Christian teaching addresses our intellect, our actions, our will, or our emotions. Few are the credible teachers who teach us about hearing God—though they should—or about knowing him personally. Yet that is what the Bible says he desires.

Scripture is filled with metaphors for the nature of God's relationship with us. We are his sheep, his friends, his children, and—breathtakingly intimate—his spouse. These are relational metaphors. And the essence of relationship is communication.

Communication is so important to the human soul that many countries have outlawed solitary confinement as cruel and unusual punishment. Yet we Christians teach Christianity as though it's a philosophy class or a code of ethics, completely void of personal connection. We treat the Bible as though it's an auto repair manual instead of a personal letter from God.

Christians are great at doing clinical, detached dissections of biblical metaphors, exegeting the essence of their meanings. But God wants us to *wear* those metaphors like clothes—to put them on, live in them, and make them real. He wants us to begin to hear his voice.

Yes, it's helpful to understand the exegetical meanings of scriptural metaphors. It's better to meet their Author.

He Really Does Speak to Us

Our Father wants conversation. He wants us to learn to recognize his voice. He literally speaks so we can literally hear. He doesn't always say what we want him to say; he often doesn't speak in the manner we expect; and hearing his voice requires us to learn to listen. But he is always speaking.

Scripture is filled with passages that teach us God speaks today. Here are a few for the skeptical:

> The sheep *hear his voice*, and he calls his own sheep by name. (John 10:3)

> Call to me and I will answer you, and *will tell you* great and hidden things that you have not known. (Jer. 33:3)

> Behold, I stand at the door and knock. If anyone *hears my voice* and opens the door, I will come in to him and eat with him, and he with me. (Rev. 3:20)

> When the Spirit of truth comes, he will *guide you* into all the truth, for . . . whatever *he hears* he . . . will declare to you. (John 16:13)

Your ears shall *hear a word* behind you, saying, "This is the way, walk in it," when you turn to the right or when you turn to the left. (Isa. 30:21)

Whoever is of God *hears the words* of God. (John 8:47)

I will *instruct you* and teach you in the way you should go; I will *counsel you* with my eye upon you. (Ps. 32:8)

God's Word overflows with his longing to converse with us; he wants us to hear him, speak with him, and have a discussion.

Hearing God Isn't Just for Spiritual Giants

Most of us are "normal" people—nurses, mechanics, office workers, clerks, engineers, teachers, maybe mid-level managers, or stay-at-home moms or dads. We feel like spiritual pygmies. *God doesn't speak with me,* we tell ourselves. *I don't have the spiritual stature of Mother Teresa.*

While that humble self-opinion is a terrific place to start, it is a terrible place to stop. God never speaks to us (or others) because of our (or their) greatness. He speaks because of *his* greatness. He loves to speak with spiritual adolescents. Paul writes, "We hold this treasure in earthen vessels *to show that the surpassing power is of God and not from us*" (2 Cor. 4:7 SWP).

It sounds spiritually humble to be like the people of Israel who said to Moses, "You speak to us . . . but do not let God speak to us" (Exod. 20:19). But such prayers only reveal spiritual *shallowness* on our part. It's as though we prefer to listen to God's servants rather than hear God himself.

It is God's glory to speak with us nurses, mechanics, and clerks. That way it's clear that the greatness belongs to God and not us. A humble attitude helps us to hear his voice. Think of whom God spoke with in the past:

Abraham was a heathen called out of idol worship when God invited him on a journey.

Moses was a murderer who fled justice.

Gideon was a coward hiding in the back recesses of a cave.

Samuel was a child.

Jonah was an intolerant, insensitive, grace-lacking bigot.

The disciples often acted like buffoons, and every one of them abandoned Jesus.

Paul persecuted the disciples of Jesus.

Balaam was a wicked man whom God spoke to through a mere beast of burden, his ass.

And I was a ten-year-old atheist.

Each story is different except for one thing: God didn't choose to speak with any of these people on the basis of their maturity, goodness, or spiritual giftedness. Many of them were less mature, more rebellious, and had fewer spiritual gifts than you.

"Oh," you might say, "but God chose them (even the rebels) because he saw their *natural* gifts. He knew he could do great things through them." That kind of thinking—and we all think that way occasionally—is contrary to the gospel. The gospel is always about God working with people who are completely unworthy of his attention. (That's why it's called the *gospel*.) He doesn't use our greatness as much as he uses his own greatness to bring about something great in us.

> The gospel is always about God working with people who are completely unworthy of his attention.

God can make the littlest among us great, but he can't use the greatest among us until we become little. God wants to speak to you (O little men and women!) words of comfort, love, conviction, and hope. Yes, *you*.

How Do We Recognize His Voice?

When I heard God as a ten-year-old, it wasn't through an audible voice. There was no handwriting on the wall (except perhaps what I had crayoned on it when my mom wasn't looking), nor was there a burning bush or a levitating tablespoon. I wasn't even reading the Bible. (Remember, I was a recent convert to atheism.)

Yet something stirred in my soul. It was as clear as an audible voice and as powerful as a thunderclap. Somehow I knew God had spoken real words to me personally. There was an inner resonance, a quickening in my heart. And I knew it was God.

When the disciples reminisced about their unexpected discussion with Jesus on the road to Emmaus, they said, "Did not our hearts burn within us?" I too experienced a voice burning in my heart. It thrilled and delighted me. And changed my life.

God Speaks in Multiple Methods and Moments

Our imperfect nature often causes us to miss the diverse ways and multiple occasions through which a perfect God speaks to us. The book of Job declares, "God speaks in one way, and in two, though man does not perceive it" (33:14). God is infinite, and he speaks in countless ways and settings.

Yet we finite creatures impose on God our limited expectations for how he speaks, in manners we're familiar and comfortable with, or perhaps the only ways we know. Certainly God speaks to us through those means, through Scripture study and Sunday sermons. He's just not confined to them. He is, after all, the most creative Being in the universe, and he communicates with us through an infinitely imaginative mixture of methods and moments.

Throughout this book, I'll reinforce those two principles of *methods* and *moments*. It's vital to keep them in mind if we want to grow in our ability to hear God's voice clearly. Let's look at them more closely.

Methods

Part of the reason we fail to perceive God's personal word to us arises from false expectations constructed when other people recount their experiences. We too often hear people share descriptions of God speaking as though they happened like a scripted dialogue:

I asked God: *What should I do with my life?*
God replied: *Are you willing to take a risk?*
I said: *Yes, but I don't know what to do.*
God said: *Move to Timbuktu.*

When friends tell stories like this, we think, *I never hear God converse with me that clearly.* Let me tell you a secret: they don't either. At least not most of the time. Those reports are shorthand summaries of hours spent thinking, praying, hearing nudges, getting senses, and recognizing God's voice.

God employs multiple methods to communicate with us; he is not a paint-by-number God. If we limit his voice to just, say, the scripted dialogue or biblical studies, then we will miss his voice when he speaks in other ways. Below are his more common methods.

A Responsive Resonance

God often speaks by nudging our hearts in response to an external circumstance. The nudge may be described as a burning in our heart or a sense of the weightiness of a particular moment. Perhaps a Scripture passage jumps out at us in prayer, or we overhear a chance comment by someone at the next table, and our hearts know something significant is going on.

For example, "While Paul was waiting . . . at Athens, his spirit was *provoked* within him as he saw that the city was full of idols" (Acts 17:16). Now think with me: idols filled *every* city Paul visited, but something in that moment stirred him.

A Spontaneous Nudging

Sometimes God unexpectedly nudges our heart to pray for a friend or to act on an issue. It comes not so much as a direct word but as a general perception, an inner detection of a movement of God, unprompted by any event.

I once had a sense to pray for a friend. I wasn't sure what to pray, so I phoned him. He had just been let go from his job that day. We prayed on the phone. He was touched by my concern, only I hadn't been concerned—I hadn't even known. It was God who was concerned and who spontaneously nudged me.

Direct Words

Occasionally God speaks a direct word—usually just a sentence or two, or perhaps just a phrase. This chapter opens with the story of God speaking to me in my childhood atheism: "I am real, and you don't understand." God has spoken directly to me at other times too, to leave the mission field or repent to my spouse.

I would guess, though, that most direct words don't come to us out of the blue; at least not as much as they come to us after sensing a resonance in our heart. Only as we follow that resonance in prayer and reflection do we hear direct words.

Unbidden Memories
God will often bring past events to mind. He might surface a memory so we can deal with its grip on our lives, or so we can take appropriate action. A few years ago, I remembered my twelve-year-old self saying something harsh to a neighborhood kid. A short while later I bumped into that kid, now grown. I reminded him of the event, and I repented. He too remembered it, and he wept as I repented. That occasion began an eighteen-month journey of repenting to people from my past, and every repentance, though embarrassing, brought new life both to me and to the one I'd hurt.

Planted Pictures
The voice of God is not limited to nudges or even words. Sometimes God plants pictures in our mind. Around 1915, my grandfather received a mental picture in which the letters KWANGSI were spelled in red letters across the sky. He visited the local library to discover that the letters spelled a province of China (now spelled GuangXi). He prayed and felt called to be a missionary. He spent the next two decades living in that very province, and he founded four inland China churches with new believers. God speaks in many and various ways. Sometimes he even paints pictures.

Recalled Passages
Past generations encouraged Scripture memorization. I was always a miserable student of memorization, but I find that God frequently brings passages to mind at just the right moment.

Once, talking with a man in deep trouble, I found no wisdom or words to offer. Then out of nowhere a verse came to mind: "We comfort others with the comfort we've been given" (a rough paraphrase of 2 Cor. 1:4). I sensed God telling me to comfort my friend with the comfort God had given me. Nothing wise, just comfort.

Since my Bible verse memorization is abysmal, it simply had to be God!

Visions and Dreams

I've never had a divinely inspired dream or a vision, but people whom I know and respect get them, and in them God can speak. Visions are different from images; they are more akin to short video stories, such as when Paul was directed in his sleep: "A man of Macedonia was standing there, urging him and saying, 'Come over to Macedonia and help us'" (Acts 16:9). There's no reason to believe God cannot give us such visions today.

God-Shaped Thoughts

This is perhaps the hardest to recognize, because these thoughts feel so much a part of us. Yet God-shaped thoughts influence the thinking life of every believer on earth. Not only can God's Spirit in us speak a direct word to us, but he can also shape our very thoughts. How many times have you felt utterly empty, with no words to pray and no ideas to act on? Then, unexpectedly, a brilliant and obvious thought streaks through your mind. C. S. Lewis believed this to be one of the most common ways God speaks to us:

> Then, seeing me empty, you forsake
> The listener's role and through
> My dumb lips breathe and into utterance wake
> The thoughts I never knew.[1]

God speaks in many and various ways. Who are we to limit him?

Moments

God speaks with more methods than we normally attribute to him, but he also speaks in more *moments* than we imagine. I believe he wants to speak in every moment. He doesn't limit himself to Sunday sermons or personal prayer times.

Many chapters in this book describe how to recognize God's voice in various situations, but it's worth remembering that his many moments include times of meditating on Scripture, watching a movie, counseling with friends, brainstorming, driving your car, sitting at the coffee shop, experiencing curiosity, and even times when God seems silent.

God mixes his many methods of speaking with the limitless variety of moments in our lives; he creates an infinite assortment of opportunities to recognize his voice. For example, take the one "moment" of reading the verse "God is my shepherd, I shall not want." God may remind you of another verse, "I am sending you out like sheep among wolves"; or he may stir within you, in response, a resonance of his great care for you; or he may speak a direct word, "You are not coming to me to get your wants fulfilled"; or he may give you an image of a contented child.

Our lives are filled with multiple moments—from waking at 2:00 a.m., to an afternoon walk, to an unpleasant meeting with your boss—and into each of those many moments, God can speak through his many methods.

God Is Always Speaking

God invites us to walk with him even in—maybe *especially* in—our ordinary moments. When we learn to recognize that inner quickening, that burning in the heart, we begin to hear God speaking all the time.

> Flying to New York to speak at a conference, a stranger said something about public speaking. I heard God convict me of the directionless life I was living.
>
> I attended a weekend retreat with fifteen men to discuss the possibility of working together. I heard God flesh out details about his dream for my life.
>
> While watching the movie *The Fisher King*, a pretty grim film, I heard God say that he sees me to the bottom and loves me to the top.
>
> On a long walk last week, God interrupted my thoughts about

finances to think about the creep of modern culture into modern Christians' beliefs.

And forty-five years ago, when my girlfriend cussed, God spoke in the absence of lightning, and it changed the life of this ten-year-old reprobate.

Chapter 2

Conversation *Is* the Point

Our failure to hear God has its deepest roots in a failure to understand,
accept and grow into a conversational relationship with God, the
sort of relationship suited to friends . . . in a shared enterprise.
—Dallas Willard

When I was growing up, my dad taught me to sail our small Sunfish sailboat. We took month-long summer vacations, and we always camped on lakes, so we could challenge the wind every day.

I probably sailed with my dad for a hundred hours before I took the boat out on my own. My dad would have me handle either the sail or the rudder. Of our many hours sailing together, I'll bet his actual instruction time totaled an hour, two at the most. He might say, "Pull in the sail a bit," or, "Turn a little more to the left." (Yeah, I know, *starboard* and *port*, but my dad didn't care much about terminology.)

Those short comments took mere moments to say, and Dad didn't make them often. Mostly we just sailed together for hours and hours. And bit by bit, gust by gust, wave by wave, I learned to sail.

Instead of instructing, Dad mostly just chatted, and there is a huge difference. Continual lectures sink relationships; conversations buoy them up.

So we talked. Dad would ask what I wanted to be when I grew up. I'd say, "A pirate!" (of course) and he'd heartily agree ("Yo, ho, ho!"). He'd ask why I had yelled at my sister, and I'd ask why he got angry at my mom. We'd talk about which books we were reading, what sermons he was preparing, what it would be like to sail across the ocean, why we felt certain emotions, and which girls I found interesting.

Then when I was ten years old, my father looked at me and said, "Go on, take her out by yourself." The waves were large, the wind seemed especially strong, my mom was terrified, and I loved it! I took the boat out alone on Lake Michigan. Waves splashed over the bow, and the wind blew spray in my excited face. I was a ten-year-old boy alone on the sea; I was Captain Hook, Blackbeard, and Sir Francis Drake all rolled into one.

Would You Really Want It Any Other Way?

When we imagine hearing God, we picture him giving us guidance, a lecture of sorts. But what if God wants to converse with us more than he wants to direct or advise us? Jesus once said, "If you earthly fathers who are evil know how to give good gifts to your kids, *how much more will your heavenly Father give good things to those who ask him!*" (Matt. 7:11 SWP).

Of all our fondest memories of our dads, how many of them are times when they lectured?

My dad made lots of mistakes, but also he did tons of things right. My fondest memories of him are of conversations, discussions around the table, phone calls, and sailing. Of course he gave advice, and occasionally (albeit rarely) I even asked for it. But Dad always loved a discussion.

> What if God wants to converse with us more than he wants to direct or advise us?

If our best memories of our earthly fathers are of conversations rather than sermons, why do we think our heavenly Father—who is better than the best father on earth—mostly wants to lecture us? Will not our heavenly Father give good things to us when we ask?

We think we need step-by-step guidance, but mostly we need conversation. And really, why would we want it any other way?

My dad instructed me in sailing, but I never felt our sailing trips were classroom instructions. Remember, my dad's sailing instructions probably totaled only one or two hours. The directions did come ("Let out the sail a bit, I see a squall coming"), but they were gusts in the winds of conversations, exclamation marks in the midst of chapters.

My ability to sail grew through those persistent conversations, sometimes boring, sometimes exciting. My dad and I went through life on the water together, and it was that simple life together that taught me to navigate. He never once used a whiteboard, flipchart, or PowerPoint to abstractly teach me seamanship. He taught me through a shared everyday life on the waves.

On our trips together, I'd make mistakes (as would he) and the boat would capsize. We'd right it together, laugh (most of the time), and drag our soaking-wet bodies back on board to match our wits against the wind and waves once more.

Through storms and stillness, capsizes and conversations, I learned to sail. Dad's guidance was present but mostly unnoticed. Within a year, at eleven years of age, I was sailing the Great Lakes solo, beyond sight of land amidst the wake of freighters, capsizing, righting, laughing, and testing my strength and courage.

Even now, when I sail as an adult, my father's conversational guidance is with me when I face a squall.

Just Be Yourself

When I was in high school, I was attracted to a beautiful girl whose family was very different from mine. Her dad was a musicology professor at a state university; my dad was a preacher in a small church. Her family visited art museums; my family visited movie theaters. Her family played Scrabble; my family played Parcheesi. Her family talked philosophy; my family talked theology.

I asked her out on a date, and to my surprise, she agreed. (She was charitable as well as attractive.) So I asked my mom how to talk with this daunting intellectual beauty.

My mom suggested I be myself.

I hate it when someone tells me to be myself. I'm never less myself than when I'm trying to be myself. It's like telling me to stop being self-conscious: I wasn't self-conscious until you told me to stop it, and now all I think about is my self-consciousness.

Seeing the suspicion on my face, my mom explained how to make connections through good conversations. She said they are like tennis practice: an easy back-and-forth, equal time split between listening to the other person's interests and sharing our own. Mom suggested I ask questions like "What do you like about art?" and "What's it like to grow up in a professor's house?" But she also suggested I talk about my interests: snow skiing, sailing, camping, history, and novels.

Mom said one-way conversations aren't nearly as fun as two-way conversations. No one likes a constant lecturer. No one wants a silent partner either (except the constant lecturer).

I took half of my mom's advice. I asked my date about her interests, but I shared very little about my own. We went to the art museum together and we went to the symphony together. And pretty soon it was clear that we were going nowhere together.

When it was all over—and it was over almost before it started—the girl and I remained friends, and I asked her what had gone wrong. She said I was boring. Oh, she was polite about it. I had to extract it from her with needle-nose pliers. But there it was: I was a yawn.

She knew I skied, sailed, and read books, but I offered very little about myself. I learned from her about art and music, but she learned nothing from me. She wanted a two-way relationship with a friend, not a one-way relationship with a pupil.

I had ignored my mom's advice. But she was used to my ignoring her advice, so it didn't damage my relationship with her. She said I was just being myself.

The way to converse with God is . . . just be yourself.

It's actually much easier to be yourself with God than with normal people, because God already knows us. We need not hide our mortifying moments. We can't surprise him. With new acquaintances, we feel reluctance to share our deepest shames because we fear their rejection. But God already knows our fears and shames. He isn't rejecting; he's listening.

God simply wants conversation.

Friendship Is Built on Communication

The nature of my relationship with my wife, Carla, is primarily that of friendship, and friendship is built on communication. Several times a day, we just talk. We discuss things that happened since our last discussion. We talk about what we felt, what we learned, and who we've seen. Our conversations lack agendas; they meander like a mountain path, much of the time without a point. Because the conversation itself *is* the point.

When I come back from speaking at a retreat, I'll share with Carla

what talks were given, what I liked or didn't like about them, how
    they touched me, and how they were presented;
how my bed was lumpy and so was the food;
whom I met and a bit of their story; and
why I am so glad I no longer travel for a living.

It's perfectly ordinary for you and me to talk about "normal" stuff with our friends. So why not with God? He isn't less of a person—he's *more* of a person. He isn't less interested; he's more interested. And he has a better attention span.

I try to have a prayer time most mornings, but I find that many of my best conversations with God occur sporadically throughout the day: When I'm driving home from an appointment. Waiting in line at the supermarket. Or thinking of how to express a point in my next blog. I say things like,

I'm tired. I feel like I'm going and going, and getting nowhere.
God, that lunch appointment really flopped. I said something stupid.
    Why did I do that?
Father, I loved giving that talk on friendship last week. I want to do
    that again.
As I read a roadside billboard with the Nike slogan, *Just Do It*, I wonder, God, do you want me to do something that I fear, or is this a
    temptation to forget my resolutions and *Just Give In*?

Yes, it's easier to "be yourself" with God because you can't surprise him with your faults. But it's also harder because he's . . . well, he's *God*. Many of us grew up in a religious culture where formalized language was used in talking with God. You know—thees, thous, and which-art-in-heavens. When asking for help, we said, "I pray thee" instead of "God, I'm dying of loneliness; I need you so much." It feels disrespectful, maybe even presumptuous, to talk with God like we'd talk with a friend.

But God is the one who told us to call him *Father* and *Friend*. Isn't it more presumptuous of us to ignore the way he tells us to talk with him? We may like the formality, but he often asks for informality.

Years ago I saw a picture of John F. Kennedy Jr. peeking out from beneath the desk of his father, the president. The image perfectly captures the relationship we should have with our Father. The president doing duties in the White House still has time for his son to play at his feet. No thees or thous, just the president enjoying his son being himself.

Guidance Will Come

Just as my earthly dad gave me little sailing tips in the midst of talking about what we should cook for dinner, God also speaks guidance as we share with him how well or poorly our day has gone. For instance:

- I hadn't originally included this chapter, "Conversation *Is* the Point." Then one day, as I was talking with God about how fun it had been to give a talk on friendship, I felt a nudge—just a slight resonance—from him to write about conversations. His nudge even renamed this book.
- On the drive home from meeting with someone overcome with shame, I told God of the conversation. I felt a prod from him to explore how he can turn even shame into hope.
- During a normal prayer time (actually, it was kind of dry), I sensed God suggesting that I sell my business and begin full-time ministry. I picked myself up, dusted myself off, and pretended it never happened. But God persisted, soon I could ignore him no longer, and now here I am.

Each of these stories varies widely by the method and moment of God speaking, but there is one common element: I wasn't looking for guidance in any of them. I was just casually talking with God, and unexpectedly I felt him say, "Let out the sail. I see a gust coming." And then we went back to sailing.

My editor once wrote me, "It's odd how when I seek him for guidance, heaven seems silent, but when I seek him for his companionship, guidance comes unsought."[1]

It's just like that. The best relationship with God is conversational. Yes, he wants our petitions and praises, but mostly he just wants to talk with us. Don't worry, he'll always provide the guidance we need as well. But mostly we need a conversational relationship with him.

All that we know of Adam and Eve's relationship with God is that he walked with them in the cool of the day. Which is a Hebrew metaphor for God having a conversation with friends.

God's Repertoire Is Limitless

When dad and I sailed, our discussion topics covered the waterfront. Sometimes he would ask why I liked mysteries so much, and other times we would talk about why he had been quiet at dinner. Sometimes he'd suggest we adventure out beyond sight of land, and other times he'd tell me to turn back to shore. We talked about friendship, humor, sermons, hobbies, likes and dislikes, and what to have for dinner. The depth of our relational connection was reflected in the breadth of our conversational topics.

A high school friend of mine had a limited topical repertoire: the bass guitar. He could turn any discussion—be it about fights with siblings or which movie to watch—into conversations about the best bass guitar strings to buy. Over time, that friendship stagnated. I wanted to talk about dreams, fears, and the future. He only wanted to chat about the best frets for bass riffs.

> To walk with God in conversation means that we learn to recognize him speaking into every possible nook and cranny of our lives.

Some people only want to hear God's words of love while others only want his words of truth. Maybe it's our personality or upbringing, but letting our nature or nurture restrict God's voice also limits our capacity for deep friendship. Like that friend of yours who dominates discussions with news about their babies (or bass guitars), we can only go so deep. Or maybe just go to sleep.

God speaks about both love and truth—of course—but through his love, he'll also open our eyes to the anchors that hold us down and the chains that hold us back. His subject repertoire is endless. To walk with God in conversation means that we learn to recognize him speaking into every possible nook and cranny of our lives.

Conviction

Shortly after David committed adultery and murder, the prophet Nathan told him of a rich man who had stolen a poor man's lamb. Outraged by the injustice, David exploded in anger. Nathan then declared, "Thou art the man!" (2 Sam. 12:7; the venerable King James says it best). David's resulting song of repentance, Psalm 51, has convicted and freed millions of believers ever since.

We know many of our faults—our friends have been telling us about them for years. But sometimes God needs to put his finger on those sore spots and gently push till we feel their pain. Only the God of grace can set us free through the very process of convicting us.

Insight

We can read the same passage a hundred times and think we've got its topic mastered. Then out of the blue God gives us a fresh insight on how the passage applies to yet another area of our life.

I recently wrestled with a problem on my website. After several hours, I fixed it. Then I read the passage in John 15 about abiding in Christ. I sensed God's insight into how I abide in him in my weaknesses, or at least try to, yet in an area where I have expertise, I still rest in my skills.

Revelation

We are blind to our culture's influence on our lives. An extended stay in France reveals French culture, but we also see our own culture anew. In a similar fashion, sometimes God needs to take us on a trip outside ourselves to recognize the unbiblical culture within us.

God has recently taken me on an extended stay not to another continent but to another time as I have studied Thomas à Kempis's *Imitation of Christ*. I'm amazed at God's revelation of how Western culture has infected me with its solutions to everyday life: the self-esteem and self-love movements and my culture's rejection of shame without self-examination.

Daily Guidance

We look for guidance in the major areas of our lives—whom to marry or which career will suit us best. But God doesn't just guide us in those defining moments, which are relatively infrequent; he also gives ongoing guidance for our everyday affairs.

While wrestling with how to write the section above on conviction in a way that would bring renewed life, not condemnation, I stepped outside for a break. I saw my wife spreading mulch, and I sensed the tiniest nudge from God to lay aside the laptop and help lay cedar chips. God gave me an illustration of his guidance and, more importantly, helped me care for my wife.

His Love

We've read of God's love, we've heard it preached in a hundred sermons, and we believe in it. Yet he continues to reinforce the message. Every word I hear from him—from conviction of sin, to revelation of culture's creep, to insight into my self-reliance—is also filled with reminders of his love.

From the first moment of sin, when God decided not to bulldoze the world and start again, he set his plan in place to win back the world through his love. The tree of Golgotha was planted in the garden of Eden that day. And ever since, God has been speaking his love for his people. That knowledge is what we most need. As John Donne summed it up,

> Take me to you, imprison me, for I,
> Except you enthrall me, never shall be free,
> Nor ever chaste, except you ravish me.[2]

In the process of revealing his love for us, God also talks with us about our exhaustions and joys, about repenting to friends, about the books we love and the commercials we hate, about how to deal with an unscrupulous boss and how to stop *being* an unfair boss. He even loves to talk about the best electronic pickups for our bass guitar. He just wants a conversation.

Chapter 3

How to Recognize the Voice of God

Given our basic nature, we live—really live—only through
God's regular speaking in our souls and thus "by every
word that comes from the mouth of God."

—Dallas Willard

When I was seventeen, while at a church youth group party in someone's orange, shag-carpeted family room, I felt a quiet urging to pray for my brother Peter. It first came as a spontaneous thought, similar to other random notions that dart through my brain: "Did I forget my mom's birthday?" or "I wonder who put on too much aftershave?" Three short words, *Pray for Pete*, flitted into my mind . . .

And raced out again just as quickly. Soon I wondered if cute Lora Matheson would show up at the party and if I could steal some time with her alone.

Moments later, the sense came back, this time with a touch of urgency. *Maybe something is wrong with Pete* (beyond all the things I already knew were wrong with my older brother). I dashed off a quick prayer for his safety and then rushed back to look for Lora.

But the impression not only continued, it began to strengthen, and soon I felt a pressure that I couldn't shake. It felt a little weird amidst the laughter of kids playing Twister, so I crept down the basement stairs to pray a bit more purposefully.

As I prayed for my brother, I started weeping. Crying at a high school party was even weirder than praying, and I was glad to be hidden in the basement. Tears boiled down my cheeks. I shook and even sobbed the tiniest bit, though I tried to stifle it. Spirituality has its limits in a high school boy.

It's Not Writing on the Wall

False expectations inflict more pain in our lives than many of the fiery ordeals we face. When we anticipate some future blessing, its failure to materialize creates disappointment, even despair. Young married couples are told that their honeymoon won't last, yet they naively think their marriage will be different. Then comes their first fight—or worse, their first boring night—and there they sit, shell-shocked.

Our naive expectations lead us to miss richer realities. My married life is better than my honeymoon, but it took bumps and bruises, fights and boring nights to make it that way. Honeymooners think, "This is the best it can get." But they are wrong, and they inevitably experience disappointment.

In a similar fashion, false expectations about hearing God cause us to overlook the many ways he actually does speak to us. We miss his voice because it lacks the drama we expect: it's not writing on the palace wall (as in Dan. 5:24–28). We imagine Moses on Mt. Sinai, or Isaiah's vision in the temple, or Daniel's dreams of spectacular creatures, and we think, *That's what I'm talking about!*

But it's not what God is talking about.

Besides, the message of the handwriting on the wall was basically, "King Belshazzar, you are going to die tonight." If your expectation for hearing God is writing on the wall, maybe a little disappointment is a good thing.

If You Expect Nothing, You Will Hear Nothing

The other false expectation about hearing God is probably our most common: *silence.* We expect to hear nothing from God.

Many of us expect silence because silence has been our lifelong experience. We've heard stories of other people who hear God, but it's never happened to us. The years of nothingness have nourished expectations—cynical expectations—that God doesn't speak to us. Maybe something is wrong with us, maybe God is busy elsewhere, or maybe it just doesn't happen anymore.

And that's the second most common reason for expecting silence from God: the belief that *it just doesn't happen anymore.*

"It's over" was the common belief a friend of mine encountered when he was on a denominational committee to write a position paper on hearing God. To begin with, the committee unanimously agreed that we can hear God in Scripture. But beyond that, there was a wide range of opinions, mostly negative, when it came to any word from God outside of the Bible. Story after story was told of kooky messages: "God told me that the church should make me its choir director" and "God says he's returning on a UFO." One pastor shared that when he was a student, three different women told him that God wanted him to marry them.

The committee's concerns were reinforced when one man pointed out that most cults are created by "prophets" who claim they are the next messiah, or at least his right-hand man.

But during a coffee break, one of the pastors mentioned that he once felt God speak to him during one of his sermons. He sensed God telling him that a prisoner in a state penitentiary was listening. So the preacher began to preach primarily to that prisoner he saw in his mind's eye. He tailored his words, just in case his sense was true.

And it *was* true. A week later, the pastor received a letter from a prisoner who had listened to the radio address and had given his life to the Lord.

After that pastor shared his story, other pastors shared similar little nudges. One sensed he should pull his car over to the side of the road, and he was spared involvement in a major multicar accident half a mile farther down the road. Another "heard" an answer for a sensitive issue in the congregation. And another shared about hearing God for a parishioner.

The casual conversation during their coffee break completely changed the tenor of the position paper. I think they heard God in each other.

It's Not Silent, but It's Still

God did a great miracle through the Old Testament prophet Elijah when he burned the sacrifice with its altar. But the miracle didn't bring the revival Elijah hoped for. Despondent, he headed for the desert Mountain of God, where he camped in a cave, hoping to hear something from God.

God passed by, and there was a tremendous windstorm, then a mountain-rocking earthquake, and finally, a horrific fire. But God's voice was in none of these marvels. Only when the drama ended did God finally speak. "After the fire, there was the sound of a gentle whisper," and as Elijah stood at the cave's entrance, "a voice spoke to him" (1 Kings 19:12, 13 ISV).

We expect God's voice to be found in stunning, breathtaking, cinematic sound effects. But it normally comes as a gentle whisper.

I think God prefers a still, small voice because we are so easily distracted by the spectacular. It's so easy to go from one emotional high to the next, but God wants a relationship. Sometimes he speaks in stunning ways, but mostly his voice seems quite ordinary, just a nudge or a sense, an idea that persists, an urging on a boring evening. A whisper.

When the boy Samuel first heard the voice of God, it seemed so ordinary that Samuel failed to recognize its source. He thought it was his master calling. The voice was accompanied by neither brilliant lights nor booming thunder. It was quiet, barely a whisper. It seemed so normal.

My wife and I went to Italy for our thirtieth anniversary, and it was great fun. But we've only had one thirtieth anniversary. Most of our relationship has been spent sitting in our living room talking about her classes, my writing, our grandkids, and whose turn it is to take out the trash. The bedrock of our marriage is the quiet times in the easy chairs. Anniversaries are the anomaly.

More than thunderous voices or burning bushes, we need to hear God's whispers.

His Voice Goes Unnoticed

"God speaks time and time again—but nobody notices" (Job 33:14 ISV). We miss God's still, small voice because it is eclipsed amidst the explosions of other sounds. Every hour of every day, voices fill our heads, fears obsess our hearts, and urgent requests shout their demands. The cacophony of sounds, like an orchestra tuning, obscures his still, small voice. Stomachs growl their hunger, bosses bark their orders, and insults from twenty years ago still scream their condemnation. Our hearts are besieged by demands, desires, commands, and fires.

In the midst of all that noise, God also speaks to us, but his voice is of a different quality. Charles Stanley wrote, "God's voice is still and quiet and easily buried under an avalanche of clamor."[1] Someone else once said, "The self-appointed spokesmen for God are inclined to shout; He Himself speaks only in whispers."[2]

Why doesn't God shout? Why no burning bushes, writing on the wall, or opened-heavens proclamation? I don't know for sure. But I have an idea.

Unlike the other voices we hear, which shout, bully, and badger, God wants to woo us rather than coerce us.

When Jesus looked upon rebellious Jerusalem, he didn't shout, "Death to the infidel!" Instead he wept, "Jerusalem, Jerusalem, the city that kills the prophets and stones those who are sent to it! How often would I have gathered your children together as a hen gathers her brood under her wings" (Matt. 23:37). The voice of God most often sounds invitational.

Worldly gods shout, badger, bully, and bludgeon. But Jesus didn't come riding a warhorse (though everyone—everyone!—wanted him to); he came quietly to uncouth fishermen and unsophisticated villagers. He spoke tenderly to a marginalized woman with a chronic blood flow while leaving a prestigious male leader to wait his turn (Mark 5:22–42). Do we really want to dictate speaking terms to a God like this?

Our false expectations of the spectacular will mislead us, and we'll miss God's whispers. Maybe his way is better.

Learn to Distinguish God's Voice from Others

The problem isn't that God is silent; it's that we don't recognize his voice. He's speaking, but the clamor of distracting sounds confuses us. We need to recognize the voice that is always speaking. When I wept alone in that basement many years ago, I heard a gentle, quiet voice. Yet soft though it was, it was also compelling. It stirred my heart to pray.

Was that voice just my imagination? I found out the next morning when I finally talked with my brother. He had been in the middle of a difficult discussion about a life-changing decision. At exactly the time I prayed, he sensed God's presence—that God was with him, that he had no reason for fear, and that with God there is no plan B.

Oswald Chambers wrote,

> The voice of the Spirit of God is as gentle as a summer breeze.
> . . . The sense of warning and restraint that the Spirit gives comes to us in the most amazingly gentle ways. And if you are not sensitive enough to detect His voice, you will quench it, and your spiritual life will be impaired.[3]

> God compels but doesn't coerce; he speaks but doesn't overwhelm.

The voice of God is a quiet compelling, a still yet strong voice, a burning in our heart, and a quickening of our spirit. God compels but doesn't coerce; he speaks but doesn't overwhelm. We simply need to recognize his voice in the manner that he shares it. E. Stanley Jones said,

> The voice of the subconscious argues with you, tries to convince you; but the inner voice of God does not argue, does not try to convince you. It just speaks, and it is self-authenticating. It has the feel of the voice of God within it.[4]

Over time, we easily identify other voices in our hearts. The voice of fear creates an insistent fixation, the voice of condemnation undermines hope, and the voice of hunger drives us to the fridge. As Philip Yancey explained, "I cannot control the voice of God or how it comes. I can only control my 'ears'—my readiness to listen and quickness to respond."[5]

Over time, as we sense the voice of God authenticating itself, we find it always drives us to God.

How Do Physical Beings Hear Spiritual Words?

We are physical creatures, and we think of communication in physical terms. Your friend's vocal cords form the words "I will stand with you through this difficult time," the air compresses and releases in sound waves, our eardrums pulsate in response, and our mind translates those vibrations into meaningful words.

Or you explain to your wife why you forgot to take the trash out. For the third time this month. Light bounces off her rolling eyes, enters through the lens of your own eyes, and tickles the retina. Nerves in the retina send the image upside down to your brain, and your mind rights the image and recognizes that your excuse isn't working. And your mind instantly formulates another, craftier defense.

As physical creatures, we expect physical communication: handwriting on the wall, parting of the clouds, a booming voice, or raised braille letters interpreted through trained fingertips.

But we are also spiritual creatures, and the meeting place of our physical and spiritual natures is our mind. God communicates to us through words in our minds. Just as sounds from a friend pass through eardrums to our understanding, and just as images pass through our retinas and enter our imagination, so too the Spirit of God enters his words into our minds. It is there, in our minds, that we hear God. (Unless, of course, you have a talking donkey. That works too.)

Dallas Willard wrote that we "must not obscure the simple fact that God comes to us precisely in and through our thoughts, perceptions and experiences, and that he can approach our conscious life *only* through them, for they are the substance of our lives."[6]

When God speaks, he puts his words in our minds, and our spirits resonate in recognition with a quickening or burning.

Perhaps the best reason to learn to hear God—to distinguish his voice in our minds—is because other voices enter as well. Satan murmurs his temptations, the world is always knocking at its door, and our flesh informs us that happiness will elude us if we don't install granite countertops.

God's voice is different. Though mostly still and small, it also has a glorious nature, and in it we recognize God. William Guthrie, a seventeenth-century Puritan, wrote,

> It is no audible voice, but it is a ray of glory filling the soul with
> God, as He is life, light, love, and liberty, corresponding to that

audible voice [spoken to Daniel], "O man, [you are] greatly be-loved" (Dan. 9: 23).

It is that [voice] which went from Christ to Mary, when He but mentioned her name . . . Mary. There was some admirable divine conveyance and manifestation [that came into] her heart, by which she was satisfyingly filled, that there was no place for arguing and disputing whether or no that was Christ.[7]

Mary had seen the gardener; she had even heard him ask a question; but when he said, "Mary," she instantly recognized God (John 20:14–16). As with Mary, when God's voice enters our mind through words and from there proceeds into our hearts, there is no place for arguing or disputing. We recognize God.

It just takes time and practice.

Act on What You Hear

We seek God the most during times of crisis: "I need your guidance *now!*" But until we have learned to hear his quiet voice in the humdrum of life, what chance do we have of distinguishing it in the maelstrom of crisis?

Let's learn to sail our boats in a gentle breeze before raising our sails in a hurricane.

A year before God asked me to pray for my brother, he spoke to me at school. Just before third period, I experienced the tiniest sense—it was actually just an image accompanied by a sense of importance—that God wanted me to go to a specific stairwell between the fifth and sixth floors. The message was so specific that it unsettled me, and I suspected it was simply my subconscious. But I was in a season of learning to hear, and a month earlier I had read that obedience is a major stepping-stone in learning to hear God. So I decided to obey this weirdly detailed word.

I skipped class (don't tell my mom) and went to that obscure stair-well. A fellow student whom I'd never seen before was standing there, and we began to talk. He told me he was contemplating suicide, jump-ing out the fifth-floor window at that very moment. He talked more, and I mostly listened. In the end, I said something I no longer remember, asked if I could pray for him, and then we left together. I never saw him again, but neither did I later read of a student suicide shaking the school.

Growth in hearing God comes from practice and obedience. Obedience comes first, but it's practice and obedience. When we are faithful in little things, God gives us bigger things. So we act on the words we hear. Sometimes we'll find their source was nothing more than a poorly digested potato, but other times we'll discover it was a nudge from God.

How do we know? *We act on what we've heard.* Then, afterward with a friend or alone with God, we reflect back on that word and our response, examining the method, manner, and tonal quality of the sense, and we thereby learn to distinguish the voice of God from the voices of sleep-deprivation, stress, or fleshly desires.

Note: We need to obey, but we also need wisdom. Sometimes the "word" we sense is nothing more than a stray thought or the voice of the world or our own wishes. My rule of thumb is simple: If the obedience required is simple and moral—like going to a stairwell or praying for a brother—just do it. If the action is more involved ("Sell all your possessions and move to Newark, New Jersey"), then ask friends for help with discernment, because it isn't always God's voice and we need help learning to distinguish the true from the false.

Either way, take time to reflect and learn to recognize the sound of God's voice.

The more we practice, the better we get at distinguishing God's voice from the clatter of sounds that shout at our heart all day long: "The person who listens to God and responds positively will hear more and more and more from the Lord. This is not because God is speaking more to that person but because he or she has developed the ability to hear what God is saying."[8]

God is always speaking. Always. And learning to hear him is a skill we can develop.

Chapter 4

What Are the Scriptures For?

If you believed Moses, you would believe me,
since he wrote about me.
—John 5:46 (ISV)

The best way to hear God is through Scripture.

There is much debate today on the value of Scripture. People debate its miracles, historical accuracy, human and divine authorship, and applicability to modern-day life. I don't address those debates in this book. I assume that you, the reader, share with me, the writer, the traditional, historical belief in the value, truthfulness, and godly inspiration of the Bible. Because of that, you may be tempted to skip this chapter—you already like Scripture!—but I urge you to read it carefully. It addresses a fundamental question on which all of our "hearing God" rests. If our approach to Scripture is flawed, then all other "words from God" will be so even more.

It is only in Scripture that we can be sure, absolutely certain, that we have real truth, from God's lips to our ears. Scripture is the training ground—or rather, *tuning* ground—in which our ears learn to detect and recognize the still, small whispers of God. Once our ears are attuned to God's voice in the Bible, we will begin to recognize his voice elsewhere, speaking to us in the most surprising moments—waiting for a cashier, washing the dishes, or having coffee with a friend.

Because hearing God in Scripture is primary, to *accurately* hear his voice in Scripture, we have to ask questions we rarely consider:

Why did he write the Bible?
What are the Scriptures *for*?

If we don't know why God wrote Scripture, we'll misunderstand his gift and miss his voice.

Let's say you give me a ten-thousand-dollar US savings bond (I'll be happy to send you my address), but I don't know what a savings bond is for. I might still find significance in it. Perhaps I'd consider the certificate pretty, and so I'd frame it and nail it to the wall. Or I might attach sentimental value to it (it's a personal gift from you!) and so I'd treat it like a birthday card and pack it away with other memorabilia.

Similarly, if we don't know what Scripture is for, we'll misunderstand, misuse, and maybe abuse it.

Scripture Is Not a Maintenance Manual

I once heard a sermon that proposed we adopt the (bad) metaphor of a car owner. The manufacturer provides us with two tools. First, he gives us a maintenance manual with step-by-step instructions for oil changes, proper tire pressure, and timetables for scheduled upkeep. Second, he gives us a phone with his number on speed dial.

The maintenance manual represents the Bible and the phone represents prayer. (I'll bet you figured that out on your own.) When we don't understand the manual, we have direct access to the Chief Engineer.

There are two major problems with this metaphor for the Bible.

Not for Prescribing Correct Behavior

The first problem with this conception of Scripture is that it presents a cold, sterile, almost lifeless image of the Bible. If Scripture is a maintenance manual, then it's mainly a prescription for correct behaviors, one more to-do list in our lives. A big one. Images like the maintenance manual metaphor are common, and they offer a hint of wisdom. But mostly they mislead us. The Bible is not primarily a do-it-yourself manual for life maintenance. (Few of us know our tie-rods from our elbows anyway.)

Yet it is taught like that every day: *Three Principles for a Better Marriage, Five Steps to Thinking Right, Seven Weapons for Spiritual Warfare,* and so on. Don't misunderstand me: Scripture teaches these lessons and more. They just aren't its primary purpose.

Not for Propagating Spiritual Lessons

The second problem with the owner's manual metaphor is that it completely misrepresents the *character* of Scripture. This second problem is more difficult to disentangle.

When I was in high school, my parents celebrated their twenty-fifth wedding anniversary and went away for two weeks. They left a to-do list for my siblings and me: feed the dog, vacuum and dust weekly, take out the trash. And don't put your youngest sister in the clothes drier again (the list included a few *to-don'ts* as well).

The list concerned our actions. Frankly, it could have been written by anyone with a modicum of smarts. Its authorship didn't matter. It could just as easily have been written by friends of my parents. All that mattered was how we children behaved. In other words, the list was about us.

That's why so many religions have the same rules about sexuality, honesty, and generosity: they've been written by people with wisdom. The authors aren't nearly as important as the insights. Confucius said, "Humility is the solid foundation of all virtues," but it doesn't matter that Confucius said it. Any sage could have written it. It only matters if we follow its advice.

His proverb is about us.

And that is the deeper, more insidious problem—really a perversion—with the maintenance manual metaphor. It makes Scripture about us. Not the author. Just the reader. It turns Scripture into a spiritualized *Aesop's Fables*, with lessons about how *you* should do this and not do that. It makes the doer-of-deeds more important than the author of the book.

Meet the Author

Is Scripture about us or is Scripture about God? It's a question we probably haven't consciously asked ourselves, but its answer will govern much of our spiritual well-being: Is the Bible a maintenance manual for personal upkeep, or is the Bible a personal letter from God? We treasure personal letters and leave manuals in the glove box.

Jesus made a strange statement—I mean *bizarre*—about the Bible when he said, "You examine the Scriptures carefully because you suppose that in them you have eternal life. *Yet they testify about me*" (John 5:39 ISV). Jesus says the Scriptures are about him—about God. They aren't about us.

On the road to Emmaus, Jesus meets two dispirited disciples, despairing that their Messiah had been killed. He says to them, "O foolish ones, and slow of heart to believe all that the prophets have spoken! . . . And beginning with Moses and all the Prophets, *he interpreted to them in all the Scriptures the things concerning himself*" (Luke 24:25, 27).

Jesus says that of all the genres of all the books in the library, the Bible most closely resembles a personal memoir. It is God's self-revelation; it's literally a book authored by God that unveils his heart, mind, and Spirit. Someone once said, "We come to Scripture not to learn a subject but to steep ourselves in a Person."[1]

A right understanding of Scripture makes all the difference in the world for hearing God. It means we meditate on Scripture to hear his voice. It is in meeting him there, in his self-revealed word, that we will hear him. Yes, of course we'll also change how we behave. But we change because we've seen God; we change because he himself has spoken to us.

We see—and hear and know—the Father, and it is impossible for us to remain the same. Putting it another way, to the degree that we see (hear and know) him, to that degree our lives change.

Knowing wisdom doesn't change us. We all grasp the wisdom of diet and exercise, right? How are you doing with that wisdom? Only when we know the *Person* of wisdom incarnate will we finally live the life we were designed for.

When we meditate on Scripture, we come to see, hear, and know the person of God.

Not for the Purpose of Mere Inspiration

Our personalities differ. Some of us would *never* read Scripture like a maintenance manual. We go to Scripture for inspiration. We read, "For those who love God all things work together for good"[2] and we love it. We are inspired, our hearts are uplifted, and we face the new day with hope. That is good and right. God's plan to arrange all of our circumstances—

the good ones and the bad—for our good, well, frankly, that still astounds me. If that verse doesn't inspire me, I must be a dead man walking.

But let's examine the inspiration-purpose for approaching Scripture. Am I going to Scripture primarily to boost my spirits? If so, isn't my search for inspiration just another form of making the Bible about me? Perhaps this approach is more difficult to discern because inspiration feels more personal than a task list.

I am the kind of person who is easily inspired. When I worked in business, one of my clients was the publisher of *Chicken Soup for the Soul*. They sent me free copies, and I secretly devoured them. (Don't tell anyone.) I vividly remember many stories of courage, determination, love, and self-sacrifice. Those stories boosted my spirits. I became a touch less cynical and a little more hopeful.

But I don't remember a single author of the stories. I remember the *encouragement*, but I don't remember the *encourager*. My good feelings were still about me.

Reading Scripture is about meeting the Author. Don't get me wrong, that meeting will definitely inspire you. It may also scare the living daylights out of you (just read some of the biblical accounts of others who met God). If we approach the Scriptures to meet the Person, we will lose none of their inspiration.

The point is, if Scripture is about God, then we read it to meet God. Let's not worry about our inspiration. God will provide all the inspiration we need, sometimes even more than we think we need.

Not Even Just for the Pursuit of Truth

While some of us are emotionally inclined, many of us lean more toward the cerebral. We go to Scripture for *truth!* None of that emotional nonsense. We wish to understand the mysteries of the universe, the relationship between justification and sanctification, the interaction of sovereignty and free will, and the difference between supralapsarianism and infralapsarianism. (I didn't make those up.)

Of all the approaches to Scripture—from *Aesop's Fables* moralism to *Chicken Soup for the Soul* inspirationalism—the danger of truth-pursuit is perhaps the sneakiest. We agree that Scripture is the authentic, God-breathed Word. So what could be dangerous about going to Scripture for truth? Don't worry, my answer is "Nothing!"

And yet . . .

Fifteen years ago I took flying lessons. I got my private pilot's license, then my Instrument ticket, and finally a multiengine certification. Of my many different teachers, two stand out because of their opposite approaches to education.

One teacher had a PhD in aeronautical engineering. He could talk for hours about lift, drag, thrust, adiabatic lapse rates, and optimal engine performance. But he had only a few hundred hours of actual flying time.

The other teacher had barely graduated from high school, but he had ten thousand hours of experience flying small planes.

Care to guess who helped me the most? It wasn't the PhD pilot who could explain the conditions causing thunderstorms. It was the high school pilot who sat next to me as we flew between storm cells at midnight. One had an academic knowledge—he really did know the truth. But the other knew how to fly.

The danger in pursuing Scripture for truth (which we *should* do) is that some of us are inclined to be satisfied with abstract, academic knowledge. We haven't met "Mr. Flying" in person; we've only read about him in books.

John Calvin wrote, "For the Word of God is not received by faith if it flits about in the top of the brain, but when it takes root in the depth of the heart."[3] C. S. Lewis put it this way,

> We may come to love knowledge—*our* knowing—more than the thing known: to delight not in the exercise of our talents but in the fact that they are ours, or even in the reputation they bring us. Every success in the scholar's life increases this danger. If it becomes irresistible, he must give up his scholarly work. The time for plucking out the right eye has arrived.[4]

So . . . Why?

We come to Scripture to meet God. In that encounter, we will find morals, inspiration, and truth—because Scripture does address our will, emotions, and intellect. It should. God engages our entire person. He wants all of our actions, feelings, and ideas, and more. He wants everything that we are to encounter the reality of himself.

The moralist shouldn't disparage the intellectual, and the intellectual shouldn't look down on the feeler. God wants all of us, and every part of us, to know all of him.

Perhaps that is the brilliance found in the opening chapter of the gospel of John. The Word is personified. The Word—which was with God and was God—became flesh. The Word was always a person, but the Word became flesh so that we humans could know the person of God.

Meeting the Word is not simply moral, emotional, or intellectual. It is all of those and more.

Jesus came to make God known (John 1:18), and knowing God is what we pursue in the Scriptures. It is in meeting God that we hear him, and in hearing him that we know him. That is why scriptural meditation is the essential training ground for hearing God. It is only in Scripture that we find the truest self-revelation of God, so it is only in Scripture that we learn to most fully recognize his voice. When we meet the person of God in Scripture, then we finally have a voice we can recognize in the murky alleys and lanes of our everyday life.

> Scriptural meditation is the essential training ground for hearing God.

If all you want is a moral to-do list, check out *Aesop's Fables*; if all you want is to feel emotionally uplifted, I can lend you several *Chicken Soup for the Soul* books; and if you merely want your intellect tickled, I can probably find you a really good PhD thesis on aeronautical engineering.

But if you and I want to meet God and hear his voice, let's learn to meditate on Scripture, and God will throw in the other three for free.

Nicholas Wolterstorff wrote, "The tears of God are the meaning of history."[5] Every page of Scripture expresses the heart of the being we call God; they reveal the tears of God for his people. Hearing God is about meeting that God. If that encounter doesn't blast your will, emotions, and intellect, nothing will.

Not even a Pulitzer Prize–winning maintenance manual.

Chapter 5

Hearing God in Meditation

Christian meditation is an exercise in praise.
—Dr. Edmund Clowney

Scriptural meditation provides us with God's prescription for learning to recognize his voice. Of course we can hear him without first learning how to meditate: I first heard God's voice when I was a ten-year-old atheist and *not* reading the Bible. But that experience didn't teach me how to hear God every day. It changed me, but it didn't equip me to regularly recognize his voice.

I hadn't learned how to have a conversational relationship with God. Scriptural meditation is our Rosetta stone to developing that dialogue.

God speaks mostly in whispers. The secret to a lifetime of hearing him lies in learning to distinguish his voice from the clamor of other voices in our lives. The best way to become familiar with God's voice is to meditate on his Word, just as the best way to spot a counterfeit is to spend lots of time with the real thing.

If we want to become people who recognize God's voice in every area of our lives, then we have to spend lots of time with what we know for sure is God's word.

Scriptural meditation makes the Bible come alive. Sometimes my study of the Bible seems dry (tell me I'm not alone), and other times my intellect delights in articulating an abstract truth, such as trying to explain the interaction between free will and God's sovereignty.

But Scripture speaks most *personally* to me when I meditate on it. It comes alive as though a deep reality is being spoken into my being in this moment. I hear God's voice speaking his truth into my life; it's like he is reading his Word aloud to me. There is a tone, content, sense, and resonance that is actually the voice of God.

I suspect, however, that many readers hesitate to meditate, either because they don't know how or because they misunderstand what Christian meditation means. Misunderstanding is certainly why I first avoided meditating on Scripture.

It's Not What Most of Us Imagine

My old picture of meditation made me reluctant to even consider it. I imagined meditation as a strange ritual practiced by people dressed in stretch pants, all chanting "Ommm" while sitting cross-legged and making circles with their fingers. I figured that its practice attracted certain sorts of people, and I wasn't one of them. Besides, I don't look good in stretch pants.

My apologies to those of you I just offended. My intention isn't to offend. I needed to explain the reasons beneath my extreme reluctance, because I suspect that many other believers will identify.

Christian meditation is entirely different from Eastern meditation—indeed, it is the very opposite. It doesn't involve bodily poses, special clothes, or mantras. Eastern meditation empties the mind while Christian meditation fills it. Eastern meditation embraces the irrational and intuitive. Christian meditation differs, not in the absence of the intuitive, but in the presence of the rational. It involves the whole person.

> Eastern meditation empties the mind while Christian meditation fills it.

In fact, you and I are already meditation experts. We practice it every day; we just never knew it was meditation. Everyone does it, from the Wall Street tycoon, to the Tibetan goat herder, to the Walmart cashier. Everyone meditates.

Several years ago, my wife and I decided to build a family room addition. As we planned it, we talked about creating more space for family gatherings, opening the kitchen onto the new room, and putting a game table in one corner and a computer desk in another. Soon we began to see our future lives in that future addition. We could imagine our lives before a single nail was hammered.

We were meditating.

Young couples expecting their first child begin to imagine the new nursery. They picture fresh paint and the best locations for a crib, changing table, and rocker. As they envision life with a child—nursing, soccer practices, and Christmas mornings—their mental images of tomorrow change their lives today.

They are meditating.

Our Role Is Active

Christian meditation is similar to addition-planning and childbirth-dreaming. In it we fill our minds with an idea. We examine a bit of reality, and we let it examine us, and in that meditative mix, God speaks.

The difference is that we fill our minds not with dreams or fears but with a portion of Scripture. Christian meditation means *thinking*. It's actually what I call a "furious" thinking. It means to ponder deeply or to speak truth to oneself. It involves actively focusing the mind on a portion of God's Word. The deliberate process of meditation is akin to simmering a pot roast all day in a slow cooker, till all the juices soak in.

Theophan the Recluse (a household name to be sure) said that to meditate "is to descend with the mind into the heart, and there to stand before the face of the Lord, ever-present, all seeing, within you."[1] It's a slowly moving, heart-changing marinade—with an added ingredient.

The Holy Spirit Is Active

A piano tuner once told me that if I sing the right pitch into the body of a piano, the matching piano string will begin to vibrate. I tried it, and after a few failed attempts (perfect pitch is not one of my gifts), the middle *A* string began to vibrate. I hadn't reached out and plucked it; I had simply sung the right note, and the corresponding string responded.

Scriptural meditation involves something similar. Through Scripture study we have *information* from God—we have, for example, the "*A* string" of the truth that God has adopted us—but in meditation, the Author himself, with perfect pitch, sings that truth into our hearts. His Holy Spirit within us begins to resonate. Information becomes vibrant.

Romans 8:16 says, "The Spirit himself bears witness with our spirit that we are children of God." The Holy Spirit dwelling in us recognizes God's voice and witnesses to it as it resonates in our hearts. God has already made known his word through his Bible, and he continues to make it known to us through his Spirit (John 17:26).

As we meditate on his words, we hear God's perfect truth speaking—vibrating, if you will—in our heart. Information is reborn incarnate.

This is exactly what happened on the road to Emmaus (Luke 24:13–33). The two disciples had attended synagogue since their childhood, and every week they had heard the Scriptures read and explained. But when Jesus meditated on the Scriptures for them, their hearts began to burn. And somehow, everything they knew was reborn.

How Do We Do It?

Most people's prayer times involve a combination of study and worship. Study involves information gathering (which is good), while worship is an expression of our spirit and heart (which is also good). Sometimes the move from study to worship feels like shifting gears from first to fourth. We need a link between cerebral Scripture study and spiritual worship.

Meditation is that bridge.

Here is what I do. First, I follow a Bible study plan. The one I use includes a psalm, an Old Testament passage, part of a gospel, and part of a New Testament writing, but what I'm about to describe works with any study system. As I read the plan's passages, I heighten my alertness, and I wait for that resonance in my heart. I read the passages *slowly*. I'm in no rush. I may just read half the psalm (I can always finish it tomorrow) or only a few verses of the letter.

When I'm done with all the passages, I return and reread the section that stirred me the most.

By "stirred me the most," I don't mean that the heavens parted or that I was filled with emotional euphoria. I simply mean that I return to the passage with which I most resonated, even if that resonance wasn't strong.

That passage is usually small. It might be just a sentence or two. Often it is only a phrase or a couple of words within a sentence.

Then I consider that passage or phrase or word. I ask God to enter into my thinking, and I contemplate. The best way for me to ponder a passage is to ask questions of it: What did God mean when he inspired it? What does it say about him? What are its implications for me?

The passage itself dictates my deliberations; however, they usually involve questions like these:

- What does this reveal about God? Why would God want to reveal it to me?
- Why does this passage intrigue me? What about it stirs my curiosity?
- What would my life look like if I believed it were true?
- How does my culture twist, distort, or reject it? How has that affected me?
- Why don't I *really* believe this truth deep down? What stops me from embracing it?
- How does this truth make me love God more? How does it reveal his beauty?
- What do I need to change in order to realign my heart with this truth?

Meditation unmasks my inner doubts. At church, I publicly profess my belief in God's love, and yet . . . I recently read that we are of "far more worth than the sparrows," and that God even knows the hairs on my head, and I instantly realized, *I don't really believe this.* Not deep in my heart.

Sure, I *acknowledge* it. I'd get the right answer on a multiple-choice test. But my life is lived as though God checks in on me about as often as I check the oil in my car. I live as though God's Word isn't real.

Meditation also reveals beauty. My friends don't consider me aesthetic; I like *doing* more than gazing. I enjoy skiing, sailing, and tennis. But when I ask, "What does this passage say about God?" and then contemplate God's self-revelation, something inside me gets a spiritual glimpse of God's nature. I sense something beautiful. God becomes desirable, and I want to please him.

Jordan Aumann wrote, "Contemplation signifies knowledge accompanied by delight . . . of such a type that it arouses admiration and captivates the soul."[2] That's what happens to me. An inner delight begins to well up within my soul, capturing my heart, imagination, and desires.

We cannot find complete understanding; God himself is eternal while we humans are finite. God's ways are beyond us. So . . . why meditate on the truth of God? Søren Kierkegaard answers, "It is the duty of the human understanding to understand that there are things which it cannot understand."[3] On this earth, we will never understand all of God's Word, but in scriptural meditation we can meet its Author.

Look Past Our Biases

During my third year of college, someone talked to our university men's group about being a man. It was the first time any of us had ever heard a talk on manliness, and we immediately misapplied it. We swaggered, spat, and smoked cigars. We were boys playing men. And not very well.

A week later, I flew to London on my way to a summer abroad. I met a young woman who took an instant dislike to my stupid, blustering imitation of a man. (I can't blame her.) A few years later she married a friend of mine. Her opinion of me, however, remained chiseled in stone.

If I forgot to send her husband a birthday card, she felt my true colors were revealed. And when I loaned her husband five thousand dollars, she told him I was being manipulative. In her eyes I was a jerk, and everything I did or said, or failed to do or say, reinforced her judgment of me.

We all have biased opinions about God, dispositions formed by childhood traumas, emotional wounding, ignorance, culture, upbringing, or training. The first objective in scriptural meditation is to personally meet the *reality* of the person of God. That's why Tim Keller said,

> Unless you first do the hard work of answering those questions about a text, your meditations won't be grounded in what God is actually saying in the passage. Something in the passage may

"hit" you—but it may hit you as expressing almost the opposite of what the biblical author, inspired by the Spirit, was saying. When that happens, you are listening to your own heart or to the spirit of your own culture, not to God's voice in the Scripture.[4]

We meditate on Scripture to meet the real God and to dismantle our false images. In biblical meditation, through the revelation and resonance of the Holy Spirit, we see God.

Earlier I offered examples of fluid questions I ask these days when contemplating a passage. When my parents first taught me scriptural meditation, however, they used the classic, more structured, acronym TACTS (Truth, Adoration, Confession, Thanksgiving, and Supplication).

Like my personal meditation questions, TACTS is a reminder of questions to ask while pondering a passage. Here is how they taught me to use TACTS:

- Truth: I ask, what does this passage reveal about the truth of God, the world, and me?
- Adoration: I contemplate the passage and ask, how does this lead me to adore God?
- Confession: I ask, why don't I really believe this; why don't I adore Christ as this passage leads; or why don't I act as it commands? And I confess my answers to God.
- Thanksgiving: I deliberate with myself by asking, how can I thank God for what this passage says? And then I thank him.
- Supplication: I search my heart for needs that this passage surfaces, and I ask God to meet them (greater faith or love, my neighbor's health or salvation, increased hope, etc.).

Scriptural meditation requires fluidity; it is relational conversation. Rigidity kills contemplation, because the nature of meditation is conversing with God about his words. So I use TACTS more as an *example* of meditative conversing than as a set of rules. Lectures are structured, but good discussions are flexible; we rarely know which direction they will take.

Meditation is a fluid discussion with God about his self-revelation, and, like a stream, it twists and turns and splashes in the streambed through which his Spirit flows. (For a great biblical example of meditation, read Psalm 119. It's a meditation about God's Word. It has as many twists, turns, and digressions as the Amazon River has tributaries.)

Encounter God

"Christian meditation is grounded in the *truth* of God."[5] Meditation is the process of moving that truth from our head to our heart through prayerful reflection. Its very nature involves something that frightens many conservative Christians: an *experience* of God. Yet the very nature of Christianity means an encounter with God.

As we encounter God when he speaks his word to our hearts in meditation, a "growing awareness of God's love quickens the response of our love. 'We love because he first loved us' (1 John 4:19)."[6]

That's why Tim Keller, a conservative New York pastor, quotes John Owen, a conservative seventeenth-century Calvinist, in his book on prayer:

> What is the essence of real Christianity? [John Owen claims,] "It is to have our minds really exercised with delight about heavenly things, the things that are above, especially Christ himself as at the right hand of God."
>
> Owen promotes what could be called a radically biblical mysticism. It comes through meditation on Scripture, on theological truth, on the gospel—but it must break through to real experience of God.[7]

The deepest need of every human being is an encounter with God, and that implies an experience of God. Experiencing God is more than mere emotions, but it is not less. Relationships require experience. Intellectual information itself may be a type of experience, but you wouldn't treat your wife as an encyclopedia of facts. She (as well as you and I and God) wants to be known personally.

I believe that a strong conversational relationship with God is his original, and ongoing, purpose for us. As God came to Adam and Eve, and as Jesus invited his disciples, God beckons to us, "Walk with me." He wants to hear us, and he wants us to recognize and hear him. The only place we have certainty that the voice we hear is from God is in Scripture. The more we immerse ourselves in his written word through meditation, the more we instantly recognize his voice.

And the more we recognize his voice—the more we hear the Shepherd call us by name—the more we walk with him in conversation, as we drive our cars, watch a movie, have dinner with friends, and watch the sunset.

Chapter 6

Speaking to Listen

Strive to re-express a truth of God to yourself clearly and understandably, and God will use that same explanation when you share it with someone else. But you must be willing to go through God's winepress where the grapes are crushed. You must struggle, experiment, and rehearse your words to express God's truth clearly.

—Oswald Chambers

When I was a senior in high school, the computer (which in those days was just a step above an abacus) accidentally placed me in the honors English class taught by Mr. Mitchell. Mr. Mitchell was in love with the sound of the English language. He read aloud to us in a fit of ecstasy, and he shared his joy by forcing us to read out loud to the rest of the class.

From Shakespeare to Mark Twain to Oscar Wilde, Mr. Mitchell took great delight when we read books out loud in class. Especially as we added accents to characters or spoke with Twain's Mississippi twang. We all tried reading aloud with varying success, often with hilarious results.

I once was asked to read aloud a passage that contained the Native American tribal name *Sioux*. Most of my "normal" reading was personal and private. I always vocalized the words, but I did so silently in my head, so my pronunciations came from how I read the word in my mind. And my head-pronunciations were often incorrect.

In the classroom, I boldly pronounced Sioux as "Sigh-Ox" and continued reading.

About a sentence later, I heard a snort behind me. I turned just in time to see Mr. Mitchell bury his face in a handkerchief. At first I thought something was wrong. His cheeks were burning, his nose was running, and I swear, spittle was dribbling down his chin. Soon I realized he was laughing harder than I'd ever seen him. Laughing at me.

When he finally got himself under control—which took an indecently long time—he stammered and then burst out laughing again. He repeated this trial and error several times, and finally managed to stutter, "*Sue*, Sam, Sue. Like the woman's name, 'Sue.' Not 'Sigh-Ox.'" And then he burst out laughing again.

I didn't appreciate his sense of humor, but I also never mispronounced Sigh-Ox again.

Mr. Mitchell taught us writing from a small book called *The Elements of Style*. In it, one of the authors instructed, "If you don't know how to pronounce a word, say it loud! . . . Why compound ignorance with inaudibility?"[1] I gave Mr. Mitchell a chance to rethink those instructions.

Murmur God's Law

Ever since David quieted the spirit of Saul with songs, the book of Psalms has instructed believers on how to converse with God in prayer. Through Psalms, we learn how to praise, repent, share our anger and confusion, question our souls, and see God.

The very first psalm, however, is different from the subsequent 149. It reads more like it was written for the book of Proverbs than for Psalms. It's not praise, confession, anger, or confusion. Rather, Psalm 1 is a meditation, a meditation on the value of meditation. It's almost like the compiler of Psalms made a mistake. He meant to use these verses to introduce the book of *Proverbs*, but his computer (which was a step *below* an abacus) accidentally saved them to introduce the Psalms.

Could that be? Could the compiler have made a simple printing error? Or could it be that God, the master psalm compiler, deliberately started the book of Psalms with a meditation? That is, could God be speaking to us about the *nature* of prayer when he introduces Psalms with a meditation?

Psalm 1 begins,

> Blessed [happy, content, fulfilled] is the one
>   who does not walk in step with the wicked
> or stand in the way that sinners take
>   or sit in the company of mockers,
> but whose delight is in the law of the Lord,
>   and who mediatates on his law day and night. (vv. 1–2)

The Psalm begins by declaring that the people who are most blessed are the people who meditate. The Hebrew word for *meditate* means to murmur, to speak quietly to oneself, to utter, or to make sounds. By implication, it means to muse or ponder in the heart.

As Augustine himself once reflected, "He who thinks certainly speaks in his heart."[2]

But we don't speak to our heart about just anything; the blessed (most happy) person is the one who murmurs in his heart all of the words of God. Psalm 1 instructs us to meditate on God's law. Here *law* references all of Scripture,[3] and the meditation of murmuring his words is a primary method for recognizing God's voice in Scripture.

I once had a boss who seemed incapable of explaining his directions. On one occasion he said, "I want you to change the taxonomy of our metadata." I thought I knew what he meant, but I wasn't sure, so I asked for clarification: "Do you want me to reorganize our online help?" He answered by repeating his original command—word for word, perfectly—only he raised his voice a dozen decibels.

Sometimes we need to use other words in order to understand the original language.

C. S. Lewis wanted everyone to learn how to explain deep spiritual truths with normal words. He wrote, "I have come to the conviction that if you cannot translate your thoughts into [everyday] language, then your thoughts were confused. Power to translate is the test of having really understood."[4]

Einstein agreed, and added color, when he said, "You do not really understand something unless you can explain it to your grandmother."[5] Part of scriptural meditation is learning to explain the words of the Bible to the "grandmother" in all of us.

One of the best ways to meditate on Scripture—and therefore to hear God—is to quietly speak God's words back to him in our own language. In other words, we paraphrase the Bible. We don't do this to create new Scripture; rather, in speaking God's words back to him in our own language, we express out loud our understanding.

Sometimes his Spirit in our spirit tells us that we just said "Sigh-Ox," and sometimes his Spirit in ours says, "Well done, good and faithful servant."

Write Your Own Paraphrase

The following is the process I've learned over the years. I begin by repeating the original verse in my usual translation. I even say it out loud (albeit in a whisper—I don't want my wife to think I'm getting crazier). As I repeat the words, I ponder the meaning of each word, sometimes just repeating a phrase.

Next, I look at two or three other translations of the verse, and I speak those translated words as well, sometimes out loud and sometimes just in my mind. My usual translation is the English Standard Version (ESV), but my meditation library also includes these:

- American Standard Version (ASV)
- International Standard Version (ISV)
- King James Version (KJV)
- New International Version (NIV)
- New Living Translation (NLT)
- The Message (MSG—a popular paraphrase of the entire Bible)[6]

(A great online resource is http://biblehub.com/. You search for a particular verse, and the site offers about twenty different translations.)

I examine several translations. The diversity of words chosen by the variety of translators helps me begin to see the truth of God. After reading a few translations, I write my own paraphrase. For example, while meditating on Ephesians, I recently got stuck—in a good way—on a few verses near the beginning. Here is how the ESV translates Ephesians 1:5 (beginning with a couple words from the end of verse 4):

In love he predestined us for adoption as sons through Jesus Christ, according to the purpose of his will.

But look at how other versions render the same passage:

KJV: Having predestinated us unto the adoption of children by Jesus Christ to himself, according to the *good pleasure* of his will.

NLT: God *decided in advance* to adopt us into his own family by bringing us to himself through Jesus Christ. This is what *he wanted to do*, and it gave him *great pleasure*.

MSG: *Long, long ago* he decided to adopt us into his family through Jesus Christ. (*What pleasure he took in planning this!*)

The differences in the translations inspired my meditation. They made me ponder the essential truth of God's Word. The ESV said it was according to God's "purpose," while the KJV said it was his "good pleasure." And while the ESV mentioned his "will," the NLT said, "He wanted to do it" (the word for "will" can also be translated "desire").

So here is my current paraphrase:

Out of his love, God chose—long before the earth was formed—to adopt us (*me too*) as his sons and into his family through Jesus Christ; he adopted us because he wanted to, and it gave him pleasure!

I pray my paraphrase out loud to God. I speak it, and in those murmurs, I sense the still voice of God quietly speaking, authenticating his word, telling me of his love, delight, and good pleasure.

Throughout this book you will notice many passages whose references are noted as "SWP." They are my personal paraphrases and translations, the results of my own scriptural meditations over the years. They are my attempts to explain biblical meanings to the grandmother in me.

Interact with Scripture to Grasp Its Truth

Our purpose and good pleasure is to understand God's Word, his will and desire. It's to know what God has revealed about himself. In meditation we meet the Person who came to us in Incarnate Truth.

We are in no way creating *new* Scripture, nor do we want words that confuse or distort God's purpose. Someone once said, "Everything should be made as simple as possible, *but not simpler.*"[7] We explain Scripture in our own simple words, yes, but with the goal of understanding the truth in God's Word, not of hiding or distorting its meaning.

We want to find and uproot the unspoken *Sigh-Ox* beliefs in all of us, not nurture them.

To make sure our paraphrases faithfully reflect God's Word, it's wise to check them against commentaries and other resources, because we want to know truth. Biblehub.com includes many study tools such as cross-references, word studies, contextual summaries, and commentaries. As we pray back our paraphrases to God and to our own souls, we echo David's prayer, "My Lord, may every utterance of my lips and the quiet whispers of my heart be delightfully acceptable—and truthful—in your presence" (Ps. 19:14 SWP).

Meditation of Any Sort Changes Us

In the second original Star Trek movie, *The Wrath of Khan*, the crew of the Enterprise faces a genetically engineered, unnaturally powerful tyrant who has escaped a fifteen-year exile. Khan is intent on exacting his vengeance on Captain Kirk, who originally imprisoned him. During his exile, Khan has brooded over—*meditated on*—revenge. He has read and reread the book *Moby Dick* until his copy is in tatters. At the end of the movie, he quotes from the book, shouting, "From hell's heart I stab at thee."

Khan became what he meditated on: he became the fanatical, vengeful Captain Ahab.

All deep, intense thinking—be it brooding, worrying, pondering, or meditating—shapes us. It forms and reforms who we are at our deepest level. Meditating remakes us in the image of our deepest thoughts.

That's why soft-core porn addicts so often escalate to hard-core porn or adultery. It's why fashion devotees spend more money than they can afford on clothing they can't even use. The heart-changing nature of meditation is why advertisers spend billions of dollars on imagination-grabbing television ads. Their video images commandeer our minds, we think of Apple watches and plasma TVs, and we rush out to buy something unheard-of and unneeded a generation ago.

Psalm 1 promises that those of us who meditate on Scripture become like resilient trees that weather the droughts and storms of life. When we meditate on God's Word, we grow solid, significant, and strong; conversely, those who meditate on anything else become hollow shells, the husks of seeds, empty and insignificant, blown around by every latest puff of wind.

Everyone meditates; everyone thinks and dreams. We can't help it. We are thinking creatures. C. S. Lewis challenges us: "You are not, in fact, going to read nothing. . . . If you don't read good books you will read bad ones. If you don't go on thinking rationally, you will think irrationally. If you reject aesthetic satisfactions, you will fall into sensual satisfactions."[8] And I add to Lewis's quote: If you don't meditate on God's words of substance, you'll meditate on unsatisfying chaff.

> Everyone meditates; everyone thinks and dreams. We can't help it.

We will always meditate, either on the reality of God or on our next job promotion. But only one subject of meditation calms our hearts: "I know nothing which can so comfort the soul; so calm the swelling billows of sorrow and grief; so speak peace to the winds of trial, as a devout musing upon the subject of the Godhead."[9]

Through meditation, we speak and are spoken to. We meet the life-changing reality of God.

Tell Others

Meditating on the Word doesn't happen the same way every time for me, and certainly not with the same intensity. Sometimes I'm stirred by verses in the first passage I read, and I skip the rest of the passages in my daily reading plan. Other days—most days, really—I finish all the passages in my plan, and I ask myself which of all the verses I read stirred me the most. Then I return to those verses. I meditate, murmur, rephrase, and gaze.

Once we hear God speak, we share what we hear. The best way for us to adopt a truth in our heart is to express it to another: our spouse, friend, colleague, or that stranger on the bus. What began in our mind descends into our heart, and then, with our mind again, we articulate with words the wordless vision of God.

C. S. Lewis said, "We delight to praise what we enjoy because the praise not merely expresses but completes the enjoyment. . . . It is not out of compliment that lovers keep on telling one another how beautiful they are; the delight is incomplete until it is expressed."[10] Elsewhere Lewis says, "Except where intolerably adverse circumstances interfere, praise almost seems to be inner health made audible."[11]

That is what we do as we murmur God's words back to him: we are praising him, making our inner health audible. And in that audible speaking, we hear God's voice.

Chapter 7

Brainstorming with God

Language is spoken into us; we learn language only as we are spoken to. We are plunged at birth into a sea of language. . . . Then slowly, syllable by syllable, we acquire the capacity to answer: mama, papa, bottle, blanket, yes, no. Not one of these words was a first word. . . . All speech is answering speech. We were all spoken to before we spoke.

—Eugene Peterson

I remember with almost perfect clarity the first time I was invited to an office brainstorming party. It was my first year at a software company, we had a client in deep trouble, and that client made sure we shared their pain.

The mix between our software and their use of our software had somehow soured. They weren't getting the results they wanted, and they plagued our help desk with cries of anguish.

My boss, Tim, invited three of us into the executive conference room for an afternoon of brainstorming. He told us to "Come as you are," meaning no notes, no plans, no agendas, and no egos. (Of course, it was easier to park our notes at our desks than to park our egos at the door, but we tried.)

The only tools in the room were two whiteboards, about twenty-seven dry-erase markers, and four sets of imaginations with legs.

My boss began the meeting by saying, "Right now, there are no bosses, no subordinates, no answer-men, no timidity, and no stupid answers. The primary rule for this meeting is: *No criticism!*" When an idea was raised, it was put on the board with no frowns, rejections, defensiveness, or denunciation.

We examined the problem as if we were exploring an old mansion. We opened every door, peeked in every window, inspected every cabinet, checked the outlets and lights, wandered the basement, and even flushed the toilets. It was a free-for-all in the finest sense of the word. We spent hours writing ideas on the whiteboards. Nothing was too big to consider ("Maybe we should move an employee there for a year"), nothing impossible to imagine ("Maybe we have a software bug"—naw!), and nothing too small to dismiss ("Maybe we could change the prompts on the screens").

One person's suggestion triggered ideas in the rest of us. Dave suggested that the client needed more training, so I thought maybe we could rewrite our manuals, and Phil wondered if we could write custom procedure checklists for them. Ideas begat ideas, and suggestions birthed creativity.

Soon notions and reflections littered the whiteboards till they looked like an eight-year-old's attempts to summarize *Macbeth*.

When the flood of creativity slowed to a trickle, we began to categorize our random thoughts. We erased one whiteboard (after carefully copying everything down) and began to make headlines with bullet points beneath:

- Ways the client misuses the software
- Features the software is missing
- Possible bugs in the software (a very short list, of course)
- Possible personnel changes (at both companies)
- Better ways to instruct, train, coach, and document
- Practical means to keep costs affordable for both companies

As we categorized ideas, we also eliminated ideas. Amazingly, few egos were bruised when specific ideas were rejected; by this point, almost all the better ideas were communally owned, generated by the creative buzz of one idea sparking another. The very best ideas belonged to all of us.

We finally condensed all of our brainstorming hours into a simple proposal with mutually shared costs. My boss suggested it to the client, the client agreed to it (without even a negotiation, which was a first), and it worked. Together we had created a masterpiece—maybe not the Sistine Chapel, but at least a masterful business plan.

I began by saying I remembered with "almost perfect clarity" that first brainstorming party, and my memory of it is still nearly picture-perfect. I still see where each of us sat. I remember Phil's excitement over a stream of thought we were riding. I picture the red, blue, green, and black marker jottings on the board. And I perfectly remember the feeling of camaraderie and creativity.

But I don't remember the client, the problem, or the solution we proposed. What remains crystal clear in my mind is the men in that room and my relationship with them. It was never the same. The exhilaration of that afternoon changed the way I saw them. I had witnessed their creativity, frustration, excitement, and bewilderment, and I had seen their lights go on as we explored that dusty mansion.

I believe God enjoys the same process with us. Years later I usually find that I remember the joy of the discussion with him far more than I remember his suggestion that I buy my wife some flowers. (My wife, however, remembers the flowers.)

God's Answer Is Often a Discussion

The vast majority of our day-to-day decisions are not directly addressed by moral injunctions. When a friend asks you for advice because he has a bad habit of miscommunicating with his boss, you don't think of reading him the Ten Commandments. He needs helpful counsel, not a moral whipping.

It's not wrong to advise him to pray, or ask God for strength, or repent of wrongdoing, and so on. But your friend is probably already doing all that; and he's at the end of his rope. He wants a God-inspired idea, and he's asking you for help, for an idea or solution—anything!—he hasn't yet heard or discovered.

So you take time to pray, ponder, and consider what he might do. It's an opportunity to brainstorm with God. You are using your intellect and creativity—in the presence of God—to help your friend. You are asking God for ideas and asking him to shape your thoughts. It's one of the methods he uses to speak to us.

While God answers prayer, he doesn't always give us specific direction. He speaks, but not always by telling us what to do. The God of the universe is often delighted to share in the conversation and simply let us decide ourselves. Not every time—sometimes he directs—and certainly not outside of what he's already told us in Scripture. But he loves to see us mature from boys and girls into men and women.

When I was thirteen years old, I asked my father if I could buy a neighbor's car. I had the money, and I was just looking for advice. He said no. *And it wasn't just advice.*

When I was sixteen years old, I once again asked my dad if I could buy a car. This time he asked me what price range I was considering, which model I preferred, and to what extent I wanted to fix it up. My dad's absence of specific direction didn't mean he thought less of me. It meant he thought more of me. I had been a boy and he was helping me become a man. He used to talk *to* me, telling me what to do; now he talked *with* me as I learned to make decisions.

I was brainstorming with my dad.

I ended up buying a fabulous red 1962 VW Beetle with a sunroof. I learned to fix brakes, replace the exhaust, do bodywork, and even partly rebuild the engine. I'll never forget my first car, bought with my dad's input but not his dictation.

Invite God to the Brainstorming Party

It's fun to brainstorm with friends or business colleagues. It can be even more fun to brainstorm with God. We brainstorm about day-to-day decisions with family all the time: *Where to go on vacation. What to buy the kids for Christmas. What to have for dinner.* Why shouldn't we brainstorm with God as well? Brainstorming with him is not that different from brainstorming with our mate about plans for an upcoming date night.

I write a weekly blog, so each week I need to choose a new topic. When I'm topic-less (or uninspired), I take time to think about a theme, and in prayer I simply invite God into the discussion.

I inwardly consider multiple ideas while at the same time trying to speak them to God. I voice my thoughts to God and wait for more thoughts to flow. One idea begets another, but it all occurs in conversation with God. I'm not just voicing ideas—I'm voicing ideas to him. So, for example, as I decided to write a blog this week, I came up with these concepts:

- I witnessed a Christian leader operating out of his vast array of natural gifting. I wondered what his ministry would look like if he leaned into supernatural gifting rather than natural gifting.
- I was tired and feeling useless. I realized that I prefer to feel *useful* to God rather than just be his *companion*; that I'd rather wash his feet than let him wash mine.
- I thought about being *real*, and that "being real" sometimes means telling friends something they don't want to hear. I remembered a time when I did this harshly and failed, and a time when I did it gracefully and succeeded.

After thirty minutes I had a dozen blogs ideas, mutually owned by God and me.

Whose Voice Was That, Anyway?

You might argue—and it certainly might be true—that all these ideas came from my own imagination. Perhaps God hadn't contributed an iota to the discussion. I don't know and, in a very limited sense, I don't care. Because authorship isn't the point. Conversation is.

I'm not keeping track of who initiated the idea. Usually one idea spurs another, so the final list shows the children of the children of an embryonic idea. The ancestry of any individual idea isn't examined. I just write down the ideas as they come, without frown, rejection, or dismissal.

But with one *absolutely essential* rule: to the best of my ability, *I reject ideas from voices that aren't invited to the brainstorming party.* Many of the ideas that come to mind, maybe most, are my own. Some, I believe, come from God. But some ideas also come from the world, the flesh, and the Devil. I want to shut the door to those party crashers.

This is one reason why it is so important to learn how to discern God's voice: because as we do, we also learn—and get better at it over time—to recognize the voice of unwanted and uninvited visitors. Those voices we absolutely must critique and reject.

Scripture is God's self-revelation. The better we know the truth it reveals, the more adept we become at recognizing imposters. The best counterfeits appear to be the genuine article, so the way to spot fakes is to spend lots of time handling the real thing.

Let's say that while I'm brainstorming blog ideas, this pops into my mind: "Write about the value of multiple sexual partners." I dismiss the notion even as it flits through my mind. It's easy to spot a bad counterfeit that doesn't even remotely square with Scripture. But what about "Write about making your spouse the absolute love of your life"? This one is harder to discern. It's true that I should love my wife, so the idea seems right. But she is not to be the absolute love of my life. That place is reserved for God. This counterfeit is much more clever than the first one, but it's still a counterfeit. We need to guard against good counterfeits. They can be quite convincing at first blush, but the truth of God's Word will reveal their deception.

> Reject ideas from voices that aren't invited to the brainstorming party.

In our brainstorming with God, let's also be cautious about any ideas that run counter to long-held Christian truths. If I believe God speaks to me today—and I do—then I also have to believe that God has been speaking to believers for the last two thousand years.

For instance, Scripture never uses the word *Trinity*, but Christians since the time of Christ have believed in the deity and personhood of the Father, Son, and Holy Spirit. This doctrine has been questioned, but time and time again fellow believers through the ages have rejected other theologies. I need to credit those forebears of centuries past with the same ability to hear God that I credit myself with today.

In fact, the concept of not making my wife the primary love of my life came from Augustine and John Newton. Augustine cautioned against making an absolute love of anything that is meant to be a subordinate love; and Newton warned a young married couple not to make idols of each other.

Talk It Through, and Then Decide

Once I have my list of blog ideas (and have thrown out the party crashers), I talk through the list with God just like I'd talk about it with a friend:

- I like the idea of exploring the value of "natural" vs. "supernatural" traits . . .
- I would love to help people become more *real* in their relationships . . .
- But I'm also curious about why we believers are so driven by needing to be needed.

As I review each idea on the list, I wait for a quickening in my heart; for that still, small voice; for that resonating string. Sometimes it comes and sometimes it doesn't. If I sense its resonance, I ask God, "Why? What are you saying to me about that topic?" If no quickening comes, I just make a decision and begin writing my next article.

"I just make a decision." Now, doesn't that sound spiritual? Actually, it is. God isn't dictating what I write, and I'm not creating the third book of Samuel. I'm writing what I see and sense in the world, and I'm inviting God into the process. And on his part, he enjoys it when I learn to make decisions while hoping in God and not in my own wisdom. That's part of trusting him and walking in relationship with him. You can't get any more spiritual than that.

Enjoy a Deeper Relationship

When I brainstormed at work, I developed closer friendships with my colleagues. Similarly, when we brainstorm with God, we deepen our relationship with him by inviting him into every aspect of our life, including our thought life. In those times, God is present and he speaks frequently.

Today I find myself brainstorming with God more and more . . .

after meeting with a friend ("God, why did I dominate that conversation?"),

when thinking of how to express an idea ("Should I tell a story or summarize a list of guidelines?"),

and when writing this book.

But I'll end with a caution: don't get hung up on trifles. Not all decisions in life call for divine consultation. Not once have I brainstormed with God about whether I should put on my right or left shoe first. I think God is pleased that I'm growing up and can make some decisions as an adult.

Besides, when I work at home, I go barefoot.

Chapter 8

Hearing God's Voice for Others

The person who listens to God and responds positively will hear more and more and more from the Lord. This is not because God is speaking more to that person but because he or she has developed the ability to hear what God is saying.

—Peter Lord

I once embarrassed myself when I tried to speak a "word from God" for a young girl. It came to me in the midst of a prayer meeting of about two thousand people. We sat in concentric circles in a large gymnasium that had a balcony in the back.

As we sang a song, I glanced up at the balcony across from me and saw a six- or seven-year-old girl sitting with her parents. Immediately I felt the slightest sense that the girl was anxious, and I thought I heard God tell me to speak a word of comfort: to tell the girl of God's great care for her and reassure her that God was arranging all things for good.

The sense came more as a spontaneous hunch than any great compelling—but what was the worst that could happen? So up the balcony stairs I climbed, approached the girl's parents, and told them I might have a word for their daughter. With their permission, we prayed with her together.

"I think you might be feeling a little anxious," I said to the girl. "Perhaps a little scared about something. Are you?" She simply stared at me. Then she stuttered, "No. I don't think so."

Her parents looked at me, a little puzzled and perhaps a bit suspicious, and remarked, "She is the least worried of any of our kids. She doesn't mind the dark, she doesn't jump at strange sounds, and we can't think of a single thing that scares her. She is really quite a peaceful kid."

I mumbled something incoherent, prayed that God would grant her more peace, and shuffled my way down the balcony stairs with my tail between my legs. I sat out the next song.

Five minutes later, I saw an older man across from me and felt God say that he was stealing money and I should tell him to repent. I was not happy. The stakes were far larger, and I had just proven my woeful inability to hear God for something small. *Was I just hoping for a word to re-justify myself? Was my imagination playing tricks?* I sat there conflicted, debating with myself.

Finally I sensed God asking me this simple question: "Are you willing to try again, even if it makes you look like a fool?" I got up and approached the man with trepidation. (At this point, it was I who needed to hear a word on dealing with anxiety. Maybe that calm, centered little girl could have spoken it to me.)

I touched the man on the shoulder. "I, uh, think I just heard something from God, but I am really unsure if it's a true word or not, so please don't be offended. It's not that I think this of you or anything; it's just that I have this tiny sense, though I know I'm often mistaken . . ."

He nodded for me to continue, and I said, "I think—though I'm not sure—but I think that God said you recently stole something and you should repent. Please feel free to tell me I'm off my rocker."

In response, just like the little girl, he stared at me. I wanted to run, find an empty hole, and bury myself. He looked away, and then he looked back at me and said, "I'm really tight on money. For the past many weeks, I've padded my expense reports at work to get back more than I spent."

He and I prayed together. He repented and expressed how humiliating and scary it was going to be to tell his boss. I told him the story of the little girl I had just spoken with, and he laughed with me at my own embarrassment. He said, "I'm glad you didn't chicken out with me."

A Word from God Brings Life

Over my lifetime, God has spoken to me through other people dozens of times, probably hundreds. Very few of those occasions involved hard words ("Quit stealing") or even directional words ("Move to Arkansas").

Most have been gentle reminders of God's presence or love. Though many also included words directing me to repent to a friend.

Words have come in emails from friends: "I was praying for you, and I felt God give me this verse. . . ." Or in church: someone has come over and shared, "I sense God saying that he cares for you." Or in small groups: men have prayed for me in a difficult situation.

Looking back, I remember few of the details and only a few of the words. But time and time again, the words were just what I needed. I was anxious, and someone shared how God cares for me; I was in a tough place, and someone reminded me how God brought good out of the evil in Joseph's trials; I felt alone, and someone put their hand on my shoulder and said they sensed God's love for me.

There are many times in our lives when we need to hear a word from God. And most of the words spoken through friends are words we already know. But hearing those thoughtful words from caring friends, friends who care enough to pray for me, always brings life.

> Hearing God for our friends can be the greatest gift we ever give them.

Wouldn't you like to hear more of these words from your friends? They bring hope, remind us of the greatness of God, and often apply specifically to the moment we live in. Our friends want to hear God speak through us as well. They want to hear the heart of God for them.

I suspect we don't share such words because (a) we aren't asking for them, or (b) we don't recognize them when they come, or (c) we haven't learned how to hear words for other people. Yet hearing God for our friends can be the greatest gift we ever give them.

How Do We Hear Words for Others?

God occasionally gives me words for others without my asking, as with the man who exaggerated his expense reports. But those unasked-for words are uncommon. Most of the words I hear for others come only after I intentionally ask God. (And even then, they do not come every time.)

Here is how it works for me. Suppose someone asks a small group of friends for prayers and a word from God. As we gather, I simply ask

God to speak. I say, "We want to hear whatever you wish to say." Then I deliberately try to clear my mind of my own biases. If the friend is an intensely quiet person, I try to wash my mind of "He needs to hear a word about boldness." (It's so easy to offer to others what I think they need. Let's listen for God's words, and let's reject our own biases.)

Next, I begin to brainstorm with God. I prayerfully run down a checklist of everyday experiences. In my heart, I pray something like, "God do you want to say anything about a family relationship, a friend, money issues, school or work, or a direction? Or do you want to talk about a heart issue like fear, anger, bitterness, or disappointment? Or do you want to simply speak a word of encouragement?"

As I pray through the list, I wait for that quickening in my heart (it doesn't always come). If I sense something—say I feel a stirring when I list "anxiety"—I begin to pray through another list: could the anxiety be about kids, job, finances, church, or retirement?

I'm trying to peel back the onion. If I sense something when I pray about "family," then I ask God which family member it might be. If I sense, "his wife," I then ask if it is about fear, hurt, or anger.

After I've pared away a few layers, I ask God what he wants to say to that underlying issue. Again I brainstorm a bit with God: Does he want the person to repent or simply confess? Or does God want to remind me of a passage, such as Joseph's insightful statement to his brothers, "You meant evil against me, but God meant it for good" (Gen. 50:20)?

It's also wise to simply still yourself in God's presence, to wait and see if God speaks a word outside of brainstorming. In these moments, God often surprises us with a spontaneous message unconfined by our limited imaginations.

This process doesn't have to take long. Sometimes it moves quickly, sometimes it seems to dawdle, and sometimes I get nothing at all.

The key to hearing God for another person is learning to recognize the stirring of the Spirit within. That's why meditating on Scripture is so crucial. Only there can we be sure it is God's word, so hearing God in Scripture is the best place to learn to distinguish his word from our personal biases and other voices.

When (or if) I finally get a sense of a word, I share it.

Share with Humility

Someone once blustered his way toward me at a prayer meeting and said, "God told me that you hold bitterness in your heart toward your father, and you need to go to him and repent."

I didn't sense any anger toward my dad, so I asked for a little clarification. The man repeated himself a little louder and said, "You need to repent!" I was still unsure how the word applied, and I asked for help in understanding. He almost shouted, "REPENT!"

My problem wasn't poor hearing, it was poor understanding. His increased volume failed to bring me increased clarity. Nevertheless, over the next couple of weeks he phoned me multiple times to tell me to repent. He even threatened to call my father and explain how my bitterness was ruining our relationship. (By this point, it was true that bitterness was growing in my heart, but not toward my dad.)

Too many people bully others with a "word from God." Maybe that's why we don't ask God for words—we don't want to be like those people.

I think there's a better way.

The only word from God for which we have complete certainty is found in Scripture. When we hear a word from God—whether for ourselves or for another person—let's approach that word with a bit of humility. Then let's *share* words in that same spirit of humility.

When I sense a word for someone, I soften my delivery. I qualify it with an introduction along the lines of "I *think* I heard God say . . ." or "I might not have this right, but I wonder if God is saying . . ." Gentle and kind trumps pompous and proud every time. You and I aren't Elijah or Jeremiah.

God delivers his words to us in the same gracious spirit. Oh, God is certain of his words, but he doesn't bludgeon us into submission. Usually he speaks in a still, small voice, inviting us to listen and obey. When Jesus spoke with the rich young ruler, he "looked at him, loved him, and said, 'You are still missing one thing: go sell all that you have, give it to the poor, and . . . come follow me'" (Mark 10:21 SWP). Even when the young man sadly left, Jesus didn't strong-arm him to stay.

This doesn't mean we can't share forcibly, only that we shouldn't share coercively. I usually share the intensity I sense along with the word. I might say, "I got just a little sense, and it isn't even that strong, but what I heard was . . ." Or I'll say, "I've been wrong before. But I'm getting a pretty strong sense, just so you know."

You Can Actually Practice This

My father was a conservative pastor in the Presbyterian Church of America. He was not given to flights of fancy or mysticism. Yet he believed we can hear God personally, and he and my mom taught us how. As I mentioned in the preface, much of what I share in this book originated in our family devotions.

After teaching us how to meditate on Scripture, my parents taught us how to hear God's voice for others. After introducing the idea of "brainstorming with God," they suggested we go around the living room and pray for a word for the person sitting on our right. For me, that meant praying for my little sister Sarah.

We prayed for a few minutes, and then each of us shared what we heard. When it came to my turn, I said, "I think God wants to tell Sarah that he loves her." (My theological orthodoxy made me proud.)

After a moment, my dad said, "You didn't hear anything, did you?"

"Not a thing," I replied.

He asked, "What do you think of the fact that God said nothing at all to you?" I wasn't sure how to answer, and I really wondered at the absence of a single word, so I just paused for a few seconds. Then I responded, "I think God loves me even if I don't do anything great for him."

My dad said, "I think you just heard God."

Learning to distinguish God's voice requires a lifetime of practice. We don't change from novice to expert overnight. It takes practice, time, trial, and sometimes error. Because of this process, the best place to learn is within a safe set of friends who can gently correct us and who will not be shocked by our errors when we squeak "Sigh-Ox" instead of Sioux. My family was such a haven for me.

I suggest we gather a few friends together and practice. Going around in a circle, like my family did, is a fine approach, but I prefer a small group praying for one person within the group. You take five minutes or so and pray for that person. Afterward, anyone who heard something shares it (along with their degree of intensity or certainty). And you try to complement each other's discernment with your own observations. I continue to be amazed at the consistency found in these sessions. After one recent time of group prayer, someone suggested, "I think God is inviting you to lean on him more than on your natural strengths," and the next person continued, "Yeah, I was going to say that God wants you to learn to rest in him in your work," and the last person confirmed, "I was reminded of the passage where Jesus says, 'I am the vine and you are the branches. Abide in me.'"

The consistency gives weight to the words, and it also gives greater confidence to the speakers. It really is amazing when someone else gives almost the same word you were going to give. It confirms that still, small voice; it helps us recognize that burning within.

Yet don't be discouraged if the word you receive is completely different. The last person might say, "Strange! I was going to say that I think God wants to say something about your relationship with your son." That's okay. Consistency is not the only source of confirmation. God is perfectly capable of speaking more than one word at a time. Just talk and pray through the words together and see what comes up.

Ask Questions

When praying for someone, I often interrupt my brainstorming with God by asking a question of the prayer recipient. During group prayer, I once prayed with a man for his marriage. I almost immediately felt God plant a picture in my mind of a sad young boy, but I didn't know what it meant. While the others continued to pray, I asked the man if he could remember any significant event or trauma from childhood.

He said he couldn't remember anything, and we kept praying.

A few minutes later, the man said, "Well, I do remember one small disappointment, but I don't think it matters much. My family was poor, and most of our Christmas presents were clothes. I really wanted a Red Flyer Wagon. I asked for it a dozen times, but all I got were shirts and jeans. I decided never to want anything again. It hurts too much."

His sharing that "small disappointment" sent our group's prayers in a new direction. We mostly just talked about how his decision never to want anything again has affected his family and career. The question sparked some terrific prayer followed by a great discussion.

The atmosphere we set significantly affects our ability to hear God. Praying is *normal*. Hearing God is normal—at least, it can become our *new* normal. So when you pray with others, act normal—

> Hearing God is normal—at least, it can become our *new* normal.

no courtroom bailiff saying, "All rise." Feel free to pace a bit. Ask a question. Share a passage. And be open to discussion.

Where should you direct your eyes when praying for a word? If that seems like a strange question, you'd be surprised how many people wonder. My own formula is, I have no formula. Sometimes I shut my eyes; sometimes I open them. I may look at the person's face, or at the floor, or off to the side, or at their right knee—whatever seems most natural at the moment.

Even while seeking a word for someone, we are simply having a conversation with God. Conversations often go in a dozen directions, and that's normal. Don't think of incense, cloaked monks, or eerie silence. Think rather of a family room with easy chairs and conversation. That's prayer.

In your prayer, ask questions. Questions are the booster rockets that launch out-of-this-world conversations.

Ponder in Your Heart

How do we respond when we receive a word for ourselves through someone else?

In the middle of a prayer meeting once, probably thirty years ago, I had a strong sense that someone present had a deep problem with pornography. The sense was so strong that I jumped up to share it: "I just felt a strong sense that someone here . . ." And I stopped. I hadn't thought through how to say this. I stuttered and continued, "Uh, someone here, uh . . . someone has a problem," I finished lamely.

Later that week, the prayer meeting leader told me that my "word" was the single worst, most indistinct, least godly word he had ever heard;

he said it was like I offered prophetic bubble gum when people expected fine dining. I chewed on that a bit and couldn't disagree.

Nevertheless, a man approached me and shared that he had a multi-year addiction to porn. He had struggled on his own and failed. When I shared that word, despite its extreme obscurity, he immediately felt an inner tug that the word was for him. He said the word resonated in him.

When someone has a word for you, wait for a sense from God that it really is for you. Sometimes God affirms it, sometimes he doesn't. Remember, these shared words do not have the same authority as Scripture. So take time to pray about it and see if God stirs something in you in response. When Mary heard words from shepherds who told an incredible (but at least clear) story about angels, she "treasured up all these things, pondering them in her heart" (Luke 2:19).

But what if the word someone offers *is* Scripture? Some of the best words I've received have simply been an email from a friend saying, "I felt this passage is for you," accompanied by a verse or two.

However, I've also gotten verses that seemed misapplied to me in that moment. During a time in my life when I sensed God calling me to speak less and listen more, a friend emailed me this verse: "Therefore, since we have such a hope, we speak very boldly" (2 Cor. 3:12 ISV). He suggested I speak more often and more boldly.

The verse and my friend's understanding of it didn't align with what I myself was hearing. His interpretation of the passage was that I should talk more, yet I was in a season of my life in which I believed God was calling me to shut my mouth more.

All Scripture is God's Word, but that doesn't mean we always understand it perfectly or apply it appropriately. Even when a trusted friend offers a "word from God" that is Scripture, we should ponder it in our hearts before we accept it. Is their interpretation of the verse God's interpretation of it?

Bear in mind too that sometimes God gives us a message today that he will not fulfill for years to come. So let's treasure his word, ponder it in our hearts, seek its real meaning, and wait on God.

My hope is that we all grow in our ability to hear God for others. It will mean trial and error, it will bring encouragement (and sometimes conviction), and it will grow the bonds of friendship.

And if you ever receive a word for a confident little girl and you utterly miss the mark, despair not. The next arrow God hands you may strike the bull's-eye and become a life changer for someone who badly needs to hear from God.

Chapter 9

Hijacking the Conversation

The word of the Lord came to me: "Son of man, prophesy against the prophets of Israel, who are prophesying, and say to those who prophesy from their own hearts: 'Hear the word of the Lord!'"
—Ezekiel 13:1–2

In 1989, the software company I worked for was suffering cash dehydration, basically dying of thirst. A multiyear sales drought had dried up our bank accounts, and our formerly cash-rich owner was scraping the bottom of his dusty cistern.

I was asked to demo our software to the only sales prospect we saw on our bleak horizon. If the demo failed, I would lose my position, paycheck, and prestigious corner cubicle.

The night before my demo, I had dinner with the client's consultant. Over lobster bisque, the consultant told me that our competitors had badly bungled their demos; they wasted valuable time by showing off "cool" but unneeded features. When the client asked to see solutions to their current problems, our competitors ignored their requests and continued to present their wow-factors.

The consultant suggested I start my presentation by asking the client to describe their current problems. He proposed that I use the remainder of the demo to show how, and to what degree, our software would solve their problems.

I did. They liked it. We got the deal. And I kept my cubicle.

What does demoing software have to do with hearing God? Everything.

It's a Matter of Wills

Several years ago, I faced a life-changing decision. Based on what I heard from God, I had just left my job, but I didn't know what to do next. I had stopped one thing, but I had nothing lined up to fill the void. I desperately wanted God's guidance. I asked for direction multiple times a day. I begged for wisdom, searched the Scriptures, asked friends, and read spiritual books. All I got from God was silence.

I read Paul's prayer that we be "filled with the knowledge of his will [with] all spiritual wisdom and understanding" (Col. 1:9). "That's all I'm looking for, God," I prayed fervently. "The only thing I want is your will."

Finally God broke through my hailstorm of beseeching. "Sam, you aren't looking for my will," he said. "You're looking for your own." His answer didn't come as handwriting on the wall, just a resonance, a slight tug on my heart. But it was a tug from God.

He was right: what I really wanted wasn't God's will; it was an answer to my driving question, "What now?" I tuned God out whenever he seemed to head in a different direction. Just as my competitors had refused to look past their own outlines, I had dominated the discussion—with God!—by disregarding anything he said outside my own narrow agenda.

We're Obsessed with Our Questions

It's not that God doesn't want to answer our questions. He does. But our obsession with them deafens us to his messages. The restrictive nature of our questions limits our ability to recognize God's voice. It's like asking God how to redo our closet while he's building us a mansion next door. There we are, out shopping for doorknobs.

I felt that God was missing the point when he wouldn't answer my request for direction. But it was I who missed the point. He *was* answering my question by addressing a deeper, but seemingly different, topic. I just wouldn't listen because I had hijacked the discussion.

Since God is all-knowing, all-powerful, and all-good, isn't there a tiny chance that he knows what he's doing? Yet we merrily control the conversation, certain that our narrow-minded questions are just what we need answered:

There's a fork in the road ahead. We ask, "Should I turn right or turn left?" God answers, "Turn around."

A ball is curving its way toward us. "God, should I swing at this pitch?" God says, "Uh, you're playing soccer."

We fast, pray, and beg for guidance: "Should I ask this girl to marry me?" God rolls his eyes. "You're an eight-year-old boy. Go outside and climb a tree."

God is always at work, accomplishing infinitely more than we ask or think (Eph. 3:20). We miss his answers because they are *infinitely* more than we can understand. God is the only person who truly thinks outside the box—certainly outside our dinky boxes—and that is why so many of his answers lay outside the little cubicles of our questions.

The great news for us askers is, his answers are also infinitely *better* than our questions. His answers provide what we *most* need; they answer the questions we would have asked if we knew enough to ask them.

Filters Shape Our Hearing

Rev. Dick Lucas was an evangelical pastor with a church in the center of London. One day he preached his heart out on the meaning of unmerited grace. Afterward, a plummy old Oxford graduate approached him, agreeing with his sermon: "It's like I always say. God helps those who help themselves."

Like that man, sometimes we too hear only what we want to hear. We control our conversations with God by filtering out whatever doesn't conform to our notions of spiritual reality. Either we twist God's words to suit us or we simply ignore them.

Our greatest need is to hear what God has to say, unfiltered and untwisted. On the one hand, we come to God because we lack guidance, peace, patience, or faith; we recognize that our solutions aren't working. On the other hand, we are dreadfully tempted to hear only what we want to hear. Which is crazy. Our current ideas, beliefs, and behaviors are exactly what got us into our confused state in the first place.

God's ways are *vastly* greater than our ways. This means that even if we were perfect human beings, our limitations—when compared with

God—would still filter out some of who God is. Our limitations mean we not only need God to *hear* him but also to *understand* him.

Francis of Assisi once heard God say, "Francis, go rebuild my church, which you see is falling into ruins." He immediately began repairing the local church building.[1] Even the great St. Francis—whose life has reached millions—misunderstood God. Francis thought God's message meant a bit of brickwork; God's agenda was larger than Francis's imagination. God wanted Francis to rebuild Christendom.

Elisabeth Elliot once wrote, "God is God. If He is God, He is worthy of my worship and my service. I will find rest nowhere but in His will, and that will is infinitely, immeasurably, unspeakably beyond my largest notions of what He is up to."[2]

We Must Recognize Our Biases

To embrace the otherness of God means we need to cultivate a suspicion of ourselves. It requires extra self-examination when we hear words from God. Not only do we need to quit controlling the conversation, but we also need to recognize when we filter or twist God's words to suit our understanding or moods.

Do you remember when God asked Samuel to anoint a new king? Saul had failed as king, so God sends Samuel to anoint one of Jesse's sons. When Samuel sees Jesse's oldest son, Samuel's bias shines bright as he says to himself, "Wow, this has *got* to be the next king" (1 Sam. 16:6 swp). God says, "Nope," and then he says, "Man looks on the outward appearance, but the Lord looks on the heart" (v. 7).

Samuel wanted specific direction: "Whom should I anoint as our next king?" But God wanted to speak a deeper message: that inner reality trumps external appearances. That single message was an earthquake in the history of human relationships with God. Fortunately, either God broke through Samuel's bias, or Samuel was humble enough to recognize his own shortcomings.

How do we recognize our own biases? We start with humility; we acknowledge that we have agendas, filters, and mental twists that obscure God's Word. Then, as we pray and search Scripture, God reveals to us the things we do not understand.

Science grows through the study of anomalies. Our greatest scientific breakthroughs arise out of the study of inexplicable phenomena. It is the same with understanding God and his Scripture. Too often we believers read only comfortable verses with familiar themes that affirm our limited understanding. However, just as great scientists study irregularities, we must make room for God to surprise us. C. S. Lewis wrote,

> The doctrines which one finds easy are the doctrines which [agree with the] truths you already knew. The new truth which you do not know and which you need must, in the very nature of things, be hidden precisely in the doctrines you least like and least understand. . . .
> There will be progress in Christian knowledge only as long as we accept the challenge of the difficult or repellent doctrines. Progress is made only into a *resisting* material.[3]

Oftentimes the truth we need to hear from God is the truth we least wish to hear. I don't mean simply the "hard" doctrines of hell, justice, or God's anger. The truths we need to hear are most often personal messages about something in our lives.

Fifteen years after our wedding, major cracks began to reveal themselves in my relationship with my wife. I asked God—no, I begged and pleaded with him—for directions: What was my wife doing that needed change? (I had a list which I hoped God would affirm.) What was *I* doing that needed change? (This list was much shorter.)

> Oftentimes the truth we need to hear from God is the truth we least wish to hear.

The maelstrom of confusion and anger churning in my heart obscured God's word. I couldn't hear anything; my personal agendas were earplugs blocking God's gentle voice.

Finally, someone gave me a book that uncorked the blockage. Later I had to dig to find the title and I forget much of the actual content, but its subtitle arrested my heart: *God didn't give you your spouse to make you happy; he gave you your spouse to make you holy.*[4]

Before reading that subtitle, I thought of behaviors my wife should change or behaviors I should repent of. I simply wanted peace in the storm. Then suddenly my eyes were opened to a brand-new perspective. I imagined my ill-formed self being reshaped by a personal artist named God. I pictured rocks in a rock tumbler, bumping into each other in a process that was knocking off their sharp edges, smoothing their rough spots, and polishing them till they shone.

I was looking for answers, directions, plans, ideas. But those weren't God's priority. Instead, he spoke to me of his personal intention to polish me till I was something beautiful. His word wasn't what I looked for or would ever have imagined. Yet the fact that he spoke to me, and the hope of his personally purifying my life—because I'd been trying and failing for years—thrilled and delighted me.

God's Ways Are Beyond Us

If God is so wise and powerful that we ask him for help and guidance, he must also be powerful enough to know and do things we can't understand. We can't have it both ways. If he is powerful and good, then he will act in ways that bewilder us.

I once learned more from a long, eight-month job that I hated than I have ever learned in any five-year job that I loved. God didn't explain it. He just took me through it.

God's ways are beyond us. For him to try explaining all his ways to us would be like us trying to explain to a four-year-old child why he has to learn addition, so he can learn multiplication, so he can learn algebra, so he can learn geometry, so he can learn trigonometry, so he can learn calculus, so he can become a rocket scientist.

Instead we simply say, "Go outside and climb a tree."

We Miss the Real Issue

There are times when we are desperate to know God's will. Should we marry this person (assuming we're of age)? How do we help our handicapped daughter with her lack of friends? How do I handle my work that is sucking every last ounce of my soul dry?

God's silence seems criminal. His seeming lack of guidance hurts. How do we handle that?

The entire book of Job is dedicated to the topic of conversational hijacking. The first twenty-nine verses give a thumbnail sketch of a brief moment in history. Then the next thirty-six *chapters* paint multiple masterpieces of people hijacking the discussion. Job keeps asking, "Why, God, did you allow this to happen?" And his friends keep telling Job that he must be a miserable lout.

No one actually hears God's voice—neither Job nor his counselors— because they are so caught up with their own dogmatic agendas.

Finally, the youngest counselor speaks a word from God that breaks the conversational deadlock. He tells Job to stop controlling the conversation: "O Job: stand still, and consider the wonderful works of God" (Job 37:14 SWP). When Job finally does so, when he lets go of his own limited understanding, God reveals himself.

God never answers Job's question, "Why did you allow this?" God never breathes a hint of an echo of a shadow of an answer. He does something else instead. When Job gives conversational control back to God, *God simply reveals himself.*

When Job sees God, he drops all his pretentions of control. He responds, "I had heard of you by the hearing of the ear, *but now my eye sees you*" (Job 42:5). In seeing God, Job is completely satisfied. He never needed the answer he thought he needed; he needed God alone.

We can hijack the discussion or we can have God.

So God, let's talk. Uh—you first.

Chapter 10

Questions: Connecting with God

The greatest good you can do for another is not just to
share your riches, but to reveal his own.

—Benjamin Disraeli

E arly in my career, a client asked me to meet with her president for an hour-long lunch. While the man was an industry innovator, the client cautioned me: "My president is also almost wordlessly introverted. He feels tongue-tied in casual conversations." But he wanted to meet with all his key vendors.

She proposed I come prepared with a stockpile of stories to fill the conversational void.

The night before my visit, I talked with my dad, a pastor with years of experience in counseling. He suggested an alternate plan. My dad said that people like nothing more than to hear the sound of their own voice; the problem is that many people can't find their voice. Instead of telling amusing anecdotes, my father suggested that I ask the president questions about his work, family, and hobbies.

The next day, at lunch with the reticent president, I asked question after question. The one-hour lunch stretched beyond two, and he talked almost nonstop. He waxed eloquent on his fly-fishing hobby. He explored the mysteries of different fly rods. He told tales of the intricacies—and successes and failures—of tying fish flies.

After two and a half hours, he glanced at his watch, astonished. He was late for his weekly executive board meeting. A board member later laughed about that meeting. He said that the reclusive president practically bubbled with passion about our lunch conversation. He wanted each executive to meet with me. He said I was the greatest conversation-alist he had ever met.

The thing was, I hadn't told a single story. Not one. I barely even spoke. I just asked him questions.

Questions hunt for that hidden voice in another person. We give him or her a stage on which to speak. Questions lead to more questions as a kind of "Encore, encore! We want to hear more." And every once in a while, something magical happens—something almost divine: our soul touches another soul. We encounter the real inner person.

During my lunch with the president, I asked what he liked so much about tying tiny flies. He paused, as though he had never verbalized this thought before. Then he softly breathed, "I love the perfection, the tini-est of details. I simply love the craft of it."

His eyes widened in wonder. *"I've never told this to a soul before. Not even to my wife."*

He saw my shared wonder. Somehow, in some way, something inartic-ulate within him was expressed. While simple—tying fish flies—the expe-rience of shared wonder connected us. A client had become a friend. A fellow human had found a voice, an ability to express an inner secret.

That, perhaps, is the real power of conversational questions. You ini-tiate conversation and then pass the spotlight of significance to a friend. You say, "More than my voice, I want to hear your voice; more than show-casing my wisdom, I want to hear all the insights, observations, and thoughts that comprise yours." You hand your friends the limelight.

We all have unarticulated ideas, a sense of the world left unexpressed; our words are locked in a dungeon of self-doubt, accessible only through labyrinths of tangled thoughts. Kind questions from a friend unlock the dungeon and act as trail guides through the murky corridors.

God is such a guide, and his questions unlock our hearts. We need someone to help us find our own voice by asking us questions. And the best person to do so is God.

God Has Always Asked Questions

The first recorded conversation between God and any human being was when God asked Adam and Eve four questions. Before those questions, God spoke to creation ("Let there be light"), God spoke with himself ("Let us make man in our image"), and he gave man the first command ("You shall not eat of the tree of knowledge of good and evil"). But none of those words were conversations.

Then Scripture artfully depicts the first conversation between God and humans. The third chapter of Genesis portrays God "walking in the garden in the cool of the day." "Walking" is a Hebrew metaphor for a relational conversation, so we are clued in to a forthcoming discussion. God initiates that conversation with Adam and Eve by asking four questions:

"Where are you?" (v. 9)
"Who told you that you were naked?" (v. 11)
"Have you eaten of the tree of which I commanded you not to eat?" (v. 11)
"What is this that you have done?" (v. 13)

Consider the context of these questions. Adam and Eve have just directly disobeyed God. Because of their actions, the entire human race is doomed to suffering, oppression, tyrannies, war, rape, theft, misunderstanding, disgrace, shame, and death. In response to such costly rebellion, God could have appeared in a variety of forms: thunder and lightning, a judge, a warrior on a horse covered with blood, or an avenging angel.

Instead, God comes for an evening stroll and a calm conversation. And his first words are not condemnations for the plague Adam and Eve have just unleashed, but questions.

Think with me for a moment: in asking questions, God cannot be looking for information. He already knows the answers. He has all the facts. Even after the fall of humanity, God comes looking for conversation with his beloved creatures.

God's questions are always designed to bring conversational connection. Just as my questions of the reticent president forged a personal connection, likewise God's questions forge a relational atmosphere that creates a bond between God and us. His questions invite us to walk with him in the cool of his presence.

We Are Invited to Answer

When we know that a friend likes or dislikes a movie, we ask why. What motivates our asking? We want to hear our friend's voice; questions build a stage on which they express their inner being. Offering them a platform to speak is a sign of friendship. It shows our desire to know the real person.

Scripture overflows with questions God asks various people. Some of my very best prayer times—times of deepest connection with God—occur when I answer those questions myself, as though God asked them of me. Answering them gives me a chance to converse with God, to share my soul with him.

In Genesis 4:6, for example, after Cain has killed Abel, God asks Cain, "Why are you angry, and why has your face fallen?" I'm not Cain, and I've killed neither of my brothers, but I still respond to his question: "I'm frustrated that I always seem to have too much to do and too little time to do it, and I'm sad that so much of what I do seems stillborn, as though my life has been one colossal waste of time." I'm just being real with God.

Try it yourself. When you read Scripture, personalize God's questions. For instance, when God asks Adam, "Where are you?" you could tell God where you're at emotionally, spiritually, in terms of your hopes and faith or your fears and joys. You might even tell him, "I'm sitting in my favorite armchair in my family room."

Isn't he already aware of your answers? Of course he is, but that's not the point. We aren't providing God with information; we are engaging with him in intimacy.

As you pray your answers—answering God's questions *is* prayer—you may sense further questions. Are they from God or just your own mind? I believe most come from God, but don't get hung up trying to figure it out. What matters is that you keep talking with God, extending the conversation he began with you in the Scriptures and wants to continue.

Returning to my own Genesis 4 dialogue with God, I once sensed God asking, "Why is it that you feel so frustrated over all the stuff you have to do?" I pondered his question and replied, "I'm not sure. Life feels overwhelming."

I felt God say, "Give that stuff to me. Besides, do you really think you know all the consequences of your little daily tasks?" He reminded me of Paul's comment to the Corinthians, "Judge nothing before the appointed time; wait until the Lord comes. He will bring to light what is hidden, and he will expose the motives of men's hearts. *At that time each will receive his praise from God*" (1 Cor. 4:5 SWP).

Conversations with God cultivate and nourish our inner being. They are just what our soul needs.

> Questions from God are pruning tools for our hearts.

Questions from God are terrific starting points. Let him ask you a question—directly or in Scripture—and you may discover a root of self-reliance growing. Let God dig it out. Questions from God are pruning tools for our hearts.

Connecting Also Means Asking God Questions

As God asks us questions and we pray our answers back to him, our bond with God grows. We begin to see reality (with a small *r*) in the world around us; we become increasingly aware that God made creation good, but it has fallen. The world doesn't operate as it was originally designed to.

We also meet Reality (with a capital *R*) in the person of God. We encounter the Living Being, our Source of life. God's questions give us a platform to speak to him, but he also loves for us to question him in return. Doing so helps us know him better. And that is our purpose—to deepen our understanding of, and our relationship with, the living God.

Almost every passage in Scripture provides an opportunity for us to ask God questions. Ephesians 1:3 is a wonderful case in point: "Blessed be the God and Father of our Lord Jesus Christ, who has blessed us in Christ with every spiritual blessing in the heavenly places." Here are some questions that might pop into your mind as you think about that verse:

God, what does it mean that I can say, "Blessed be God"? Does it mean I can bless you? Or that you *are* blessed? Or that I wish you to be blessed?

How have you blessed me "with every spiritual blessing"? I rarely
sense so complete a blessing in my life. What am I missing here?
And what does "in the heavenly places" mean? Does it mean I get
none of those blessings until I get to heaven, or something else?
Help me.

As you ask such questions of God, and as God asks questions of you,
there is a connection. You reveal your deepest self, and in response he
reveals himself more deeply to you. Connecting with God through conversational Q and A creates a personal intimacy with the Creator of the
universe.

Any questions?

Chapter 11

Cultivating a Holy Curiosity

Never lose a holy curiosity.
—Albert Einstein

The reputation of *curiosity* has been smeared by modern-day safety police. Apparently curiosity didn't play nicely with the house cat. And that's too bad. A little-known method of hearing God is to cultivate our curiosities—plowing, planting, and watering them into prayers.

Perhaps curiosity's reputation has gotten tarnished because its existence reminds us of our ignorance. Besides, anything that intrigues us also tantalizes us, maybe tempting us to perilous pursuits. Einstein, however, urged us to embrace the exploration of what we do not understand:

> Curiosity has its own reason for existing. One cannot help but be in awe when he contemplates the mysteries of . . . life. It is enough if one tries merely to comprehend a little of this mystery every day. Never lose a holy curiosity.[1]

An increased sense of inquisitiveness will drive us to seek God's voice. So let's resurrect our sensitivity to mystery. In our God-designed whodunit moments of everyday life, we find clues to the mysteries of life, stories written by God.

God's Words Are Sometimes Confusing

Twenty-five years ago, while praying for a man, I heard a word that I think was from God. But it was so weird and potentially painful that I didn't share it with the man. And then it began to haunt me.

At the time, I belonged to a Christian group with worldwide influence. We felt called by God to explore the meaning of Christian community, a concept that implies, at the very least, closeness between people. Community must mean more than plastic smiles on a Sunday morning. Somehow each of our lives should enrich others and even convict them at times. Somehow each person's gifting should bring unexpected life to everyone else—"unexpected" because the foot has no clue what the hand can do.

One summer afternoon, after an ordinary prayer meeting, one of the men asked a few of us to pray with him about a personal struggle. As I prayed, a sadness enveloped me, almost a grief. It felt ominous, like when you're on a road trip and there's a funny noise in the car engine but no warning light. And then I literally heard these words in my mind (which I believe came from God): "If this man leaves the community, no one will notice. All will continue without him as though he'd never been a member. His unique gifting was never appreciated. *And that is a tragedy.*"

I looked at this unhappy man and couldn't bring myself to share such a depressing word. As I prayed to understand, I felt I wasn't called to share it. (Phew! I was glad for that. I had no desire to declare to this man, "Your life to date is of no significance whatsoever.")

But I couldn't shake the sense of God's voice in this message of clouds and thick darkness.

We Need Curiosity

Our souls are built for exploration, for the cognitive thrill of probing the mysterious. We eagerly devour stories of treasure hunters and space expeditions ("To boldly go where no man has gone before"). Yet too much of our lives is routine: we rise, eat, go to work, pacify an angry client, drive home, eat, watch a movie, and sleep. Tomorrow we do it all again. Ten years disappear in *Star Trek* reruns.

But routine is merely nature's respite, a needed rest to equip us for an exploration of the unknown. Puzzles stir our curiosity. It is in mysteries that we come alive. When routine rules our waking moments, our lives become boring.

Curiosity conquers that boredom.

Real knowledge doesn't come from looking over the shoulders of pioneers to read their diaries. Real knowledge comes from hitting the trail so that our own diaries overflow with discoveries. It comes from learning to ride a bike, conquering a language, starting a business, crafting a poem, and learning to fly. Real knowledge is an adventure into the unknown. Wikipedia costs us nothing to use. But real knowledge requires personal investment; it's a hard-fought victory, the triumph of curiosity over monotony.

Boredom is the curse of the Western world. With thousands of years of history at our fingertips, we feel the dullness of nothing to do. Ian Leslie urges us to keep curiosity alive. He writes, "Digital technologies are severing the link between effort and mental exploration. By making it easier for us to find answers, the Web threatens habits of deeper inquiry."[2]

> Only when the question "Why?" sends us on expeditions of personal discovery do our minds feast and our souls feel satisfied.

The dreary monotony of nothingness dulls our heart. There's no lasting excitement. Quick answers shortcut the adventures of inquiring pursuit. We satisfy our curiosity thirst with the mini thrills of small adventures—a night of Netflix or a trip to Wikipedia. Tomorrow we're wearied by the emptiness of our pointless life.

It's why we hate know-it-alls (except when they are us). Our inquisitive, exploratory discussion into the unknown is smothered by the soulless torpor of a know-it-all's flaccid facts. We've replaced the staggering roar and thunder of lightning with the flicker of a lightning bug.

Tame, tepid, instant-answer Google can't save us from the tedium of meaningless information. Only when the question "Why?" sends us on expeditions of personal discovery do our minds feast and our souls feel satisfied.

God Stirred My Curiosity Pot

I never shared my discouraging word with the man who wanted prayer. In fact, I didn't tell a soul for twenty years. I kept it silent and hidden.

But not forgotten. The disturbing memory came uninvited in the middle of sleepless nights and accompanied me on business trips to Europe. It didn't make sense. I couldn't wrap my mind around what God meant.

I was preoccupied by the deep darkness of some unknown truth. It intrigued and scared me. I probably obsessed over it. It caused me to reexamine all my perceptions of community and leadership. Especially leadership.

It wasn't that the man in question lacked value; it was that we never wondered among ourselves what God's value in him should mean to us. I began to ask myself, "How would leadership act if we asked ourselves, '*Why*? Why did God bring us each person?'"

I reconsidered all my beliefs about Christian leadership. Should we approach leadership the same way the world teaches it? Scripture describes the ideal leader as, "He raises up the poor from the dust; he lifts the needy from the [ashes]" (1 Sam. 2:8). But instead of raising up the poor, we Christian leaders read books on organizational structures, fiscal responsibility, and ways to run efficient meetings.

Businesses spend billions on branding; they form committees, interview clients, examine their products, and paint a picture of their mission. Churches do the same thing, except we add prayer. We form committees, talk with parishioners, examine our programs. And pray. It's like our approach to leadership is to adopt the business model and baptize it with a simple sprinkling of prayer.

What if there is a different way? What if God speaks his vision through the members he brings us? As a kid, my friends and I would solve puzzles by hiding the picture and then examining each of the pieces. The final picture emerged slowly, piece by piece. What if the living body of Christ on earth isn't built with dead human systems at all, but with the "living stones" described in 1 Peter 2:5?

I wonder if Christian leadership should work like that. Not just implementing our committee-picture of God's vision—often placing round pegs in square holes to make them fit—but seeing God's vision for each body emerge in the puzzle pieces we call our members.

The curious case of an undervalued man drove me to seek God's voice.

Is my dream of Christian leadership right? I'm not sure, but I don't think it's all wrong. The world, both Christian and secular, would be hugely better if its leaders looked to the individual value of each member of their communities.

This vision of leadership only came to me when I explored a mystery. The incident with the unvalued man created a heightened awareness of how little I know. I had learned many of the *whats* of life, but I became increasingly conscious of how little I knew the *whys*. I began to take my improved curiosity to God.

For example, the whys of my hurts.

Let Your Emotions Stir Your Curiosity

As a business executive, I disappointed people every day. Clients were upset when I forgot to return calls, employees disliked our limited retirement options, and other executives abhorred my suggestion to increase our retirement options. Daily decisions always disappointed somebody. And for the most part, I was perfectly fine with making unpopular choices and my occasional—perhaps frequent—mistakes.

I did what I could, and I could live happily if I never won the annual popularity contest.

But life at home didn't work the same way. If my wife thought my child-discipline suggestion was unwise, I felt stupid. Sometimes angry. If I wanted to hire out a household chore but my wife wanted me to do it, I felt unappreciated. *Doesn't she know how hard I work at the office?*

I was aware of my emotional reactions to my wife, and I tried to behave properly (just be nice and don't pout), but I never wondered *why* I responded as I did. I could effortlessly shrug off coworker disappointments, but even a shadow of my wife's displeasure upset me.

One day I inadvertently neglected a promise to my wife (again), and her disappointment sent me into an emotional tailspin. She was fine with my apology, but the displeasure I caused her wouldn't let go. My heart lashed my soul with the whip of my own negligence.

And something in my curiosity awakened. I could make a business mistake and feel bad but not overcome, but distressing my wife overwhelmed me. Why was that? I turned my baffling emotions into prayer. Why was one situation bearable while the other was intolerable?

I felt God ask me a question in return: Why was I so fearful of disappointing my wife?

I thought, "I don't like to hurt her feelings." But that answer didn't satisfy me, much less God. The truth was, I didn't want to hurt my wife's feelings because it hurt my own feelings to think I was an insensitive jerk. In other words, my emotional response was all about me.

All the other reasons I could think of were equally self-justifying. Then, in my newly awakened curiosity, God spoke to me about my self-centeredness.

Let Your Emotions Drive You to God

Emotions are always *responses*. We are angry because a boss stole our idea; we are sad because a girlfriend dumped us; we are happy because our team won the Super Bowl; we are scared that our friends will discover our dark, hidden secrets.

Emotions are reactions to surprises, disappointments, snubs, and accomplishments. Emotions are the direct result of challenges to, or the attainment of, our hopes, desires, loves, and beliefs.

> If our desire is financial freedom, any unplanned bill will make us sad and every pay raise will make us glad.
> If our greatest hope is the success of our kids, anyone who thwarts them will make us angry, and every teacher who helps them will cheer us up.

If emotions are responses to beliefs (hopes, desires, and loves), then they leave a breadcrumb trail to our inner life. They offer an opportunity for curiosity, a chance to explore with God. We can't do it without him. We are all blind to the deep things of our own hearts; we need him to open the eyes of our heart—not just to our known beliefs and hopes, but also to our deepest, unknown longings.

In his book *Reexamining Conscience*, John Carmody suggests that in doing a personal investigation of our lives, "we do well to fix our attention on the things that count, on the projects, persons and episodes *that have left an emotional trace.*"[3]

I was sad when I disappointed work colleagues, but I was devastated when I disappointed my wife. The breadcrumb trail led me to a hidden belief of my heart: I believed that all my happiness rested on my self-perceived ability to do what only God can do.

On the surface, I would have told you I only needed God's love. But God pointed out that, at a deeper level, I was a functional idolater. I gave lip service to God, but my emotions pointed to my service of a different god, the god of *feeling-good-about-myself*, whom I consistently failed.

We overlook the opportunity to hear God when we fail to bring our emotional curiosities to him. Once we learn this practice, we find his voice in moments we never before expected:

A movie stirs us, and we ask God, "Why? What about that scene made me teary-eyed?"

A daughter flunks a class and we are devastated. We ask God, "Why is my happiness tied to the momentary successes of my children?"

Our spouse never drops his or her repulsive habits, and we are angry. We ask God, "Why am I more concerned with my mate's actions than with my own?"

Sometimes God reveals hidden, destructive beliefs in our hearts. Sometimes he reveals good, God-given desires. And sometimes he reveals his personal design for our lives.

Years ago a doctor friend of mine shared how he was drawn to sci-fi movies, computer-oriented documentaries, and high-tech magazines. When he read or watched them, he felt good, while when he went to his medical practice, he felt frustrated. Over time he took these curious emotions to God, and he felt God say that his heart was designed for technological mysteries far more than for medical marvels.

My friend took programming classes, changed careers, and the last I heard of him, he was a programmer who wrote software for hospitals. And he loved going to work.

We jeopardize the very course of our lives when we ignore emotional curiosities. Wiser by far to bring them to God in prayer.

God Teaches Us Through Our Curiosity

The single biggest mystery franchise of all time is Arthur Conan Doyle's Sherlock Holmes. But Holmes himself is an enigma. When he has no mystery to examine, his life is filled with boredom, and he uses cocaine as an artificial stimulant.

We are like Sherlock Holmes, designed to seek out mysteries in conversations with God. We neglect the mysterious at great peril. We numb our boredom with addictions. That's why C. S. Lewis's senior devil instructs his junior devil to rid his "subject" of curiosity: "The attack has a much better chance of success when the man's whole inner world is drab and cold and empty."[4]

I believe God tickles our curiosity to drive us to him for mutual exploration. We seek his understanding of things that mystify us. These opportunities arise constantly, just as they did for Jesus's disciples:

- The disciples saw a man born blind, and they asked Jesus whose fault it was. Jesus said the man was born to be a display of God's splendor.
- Jesus washed the disciples' feet, and this baffling, unnatural reversal of tradition drove Peter crazy. The whole life of Jesus displayed the curious nature of the gospel as it exhibited the unnatural—to humans—grace of God.
- An expert in the law, wanting to understand the summary of the law, asked Jesus what constitutes a neighbor. And we get the perplexing parable of the mysterious good Samaritan.

Curiosity may kill the cat, but it awakens the believer. Our growing fascination creates opportunities to seek God's voice. Wherever we are faced with mysteries, curiosities, oddities, or wonders, Oswald Chambers offers this simple instruction:

Get into the habit of saying, "Speak, Lord," and life will become a romance.[5]

Chapter 12

"How Can I Know It's God's Voice?"

*Beloved, do not believe every spirit, but test the
spirits to see whether they are from God.*
—1 John 4:1

Several years ago, I was invited to join a small group of men for a retreat in the Rockies. Each of the attendees was separately involved in men's ministries. The purpose of the small retreat was to consider the benefits of working more closely together. We wanted to explore the proverb,

> Though one man alone is easily overpowered, two can defend themselves, and a three-strand cord is not easily broken. (Eccl. 4:12 SWP)

I accepted the invitation, but with a trace of reluctance. Mutual support is valuable, but I have attended too many men's retreats that involved excessive machismo or undue swaggering, and then I find myself blustering about as well. I dislike it in me even more than I dislike it in others.

The atmosphere was as I anticipated: good discussion, but too much male-strutting for my tastes. And I didn't develop any deep friendships.

Six months later, the group met a second time, and they invited me again. My sprinkling of reluctance had become a rainstorm, but I prayed a little, felt a slight nudge to attend, and accepted. My experience of this second weekend was just like the first. I left the second retreat with a strong resolve to "just say no" if they ever asked me again.

A few months later I received my third invitation. Pulling out a pad of paper, I wrote at the top of the first page, "Reasons Not to Attend This Retreat." Then I performed a quick brain-dump. The result was a dozen good reasons to decline. Never have words flowed from my pen with such eloquence and ease. (I'm looking at that document as I write this chapter.)

That evening my wife probed me about my plans for the retreat. She asked, "What does your heart say?" I replied, "My heart says, 'Stay the hell away.'"

That night I barely slept. Lying wide awake, thoughts racing through my mind, I felt a strong pull from God to attend and a strong pull from my wishes to stay away. The next morning I woke up and bought another plane ticket. Reluctantly, I was bound for Colorado yet again.

Hearing God's word had sparked confusion in me:

- I *strongly* disliked the idea of attending the retreat again.
- When I sensed God's direction to go, it disturbed me.
- My dozen reasons not to attend were still valid, and I felt no peace about going.
- After buying the ticket, I still felt regret at the thought of yet another macho weekend.

But attend I did, and on this retreat I felt a downpour of God's presence. It was on that third retreat that I felt God call me to start writing; it was on that retreat that I felt drawn to deeply pursue—and to name my website—*Beliefs of the Heart*; and it was then that I felt God give me a glimpse of his calling for me.

Before the retreat, God's voice disturbed me. Afterward, I was glad I had obeyed.

Just Don't Expect Inner Peace

Flash back to an earlier retreat, this one sponsored by my charismatic, high-school-aged prayer group when I was fifteen or sixteen. We had invited an older man to speak to us on Hearing God. (If I remember correctly, the "older man" was a third-year college student.) When someone asked him, "How we can *know* that it's God's voice that we hear?" he taught us this simple formula:

> "You will always recognize God's voice by the great peace you feel."

In the forty years since that teaching, his wise advice has been instrumental in confirming God's voice to me exactly zero times. (Well, maybe I had peace once, but I'm still not sure it was actually God's voice that single, solitary time.)

The "peace" advice is the dominant teaching I encounter when it comes to verifying God's voice. But I think it's misleading. In all the biblical accounts of men and women who hear God's word, their principal emotion is fear not peace; that's why all the messengers have to exclaim, "Fear not!"

God's voice may be accompanied by an inner assurance, but our first response is not always inner tranquility. Joy comes when God tells me of his love, but he also convicts me of sin or asks me to repent to someone. My own initial response to God's voice is often an inner disturbance. And I'm not alone.

- When God spoke to Moses in the burning bush, Moses's first response was, "No way."
- When the boy Samuel heard God's word about Eli's sons, he lay awake scared all night.
- When Isaiah heard God's voice, he exclaimed, "Woe is me!"
- When Jonah heard God's voice, he ran in the opposite direction.

Very common responses to God's word include disinclination, confusion, disturbance, and fear. Just imagine poor Hosea's "inner peace" when God told him to marry a whore (Hos. 1:2–3).

But if peace isn't the earmark of authenticity, then what reassurances can we count on that the voice we hear is God's?

How Certain Can We Be?

After that Hearing God retreat, my charismatic prayer group went through an awkward super-spiritual phase. To use a deep theological term, we went whacky. Some members began to consult God before they moved a muscle. In the morning, they'd ask him if it was time to get up. Once they were up, they'd ask him which shirt to wear. For breakfast, they'd inquire whether they should eat Grape-Nuts or Corn Flakes.

No wonder much of the church is dubious about those of us who "hear God." Too many of us act like screwballs (another theological term). The prayer group's leadership recognized the absurdity of the group's behavior and finally made an announcement to address our hyper-obsession with divine direction:

> Our level of certainty that God has spoken to us is proportional to the degree with which that word conforms to Scripture.

I suspect that if you are reading this book—at least if you've made it this far—you believe that Scripture is God's Word. You *know* it. You are certain. (Though perhaps you, like the father in Mark 9, sometimes say, "I believe; help my unbelief.") Scripture is the one resource in which we can have absolute certainty that God has spoken.

So when I was ten years old and God spoke to me, saying, "Sam, I am real, and you don't understand," I could know that those words were true because they are completely confirmed by Scripture. God *is* real, and I don't fully understand him; the Bible makes that plain.

But at the age of twenty-four, when I thought God directed me to leave the mission field I was serving, how could I *know* that God was speaking to me? The answer is, *I couldn't know.* In that kind of a situation, we may have a high level of confidence, but a word to "leave the mission field" does not conform to Scripture with the same precision as "I am real." I couldn't have the same level of confidence that it came from God. In other words, *we cannot have the certainty we want.* As Paul wrote, "For now we see in a mirror dimly" (1 Cor. 13:12).

Yikes! Here I am writing a book on hearing God while at the same time admitting that we can't know that we've actually heard his voice.

What, then, is the use of trying? Why bother to learn to hear God if we can't be sure it is God's voice?

My answer: It's not such a big deal. Every decision we make is accompanied by a degree of uncertainty. Should we marry this person we love? We don't know. Should we get married at all? We don't know. Should we buy this house or that house? We don't know. Should we take the freeway or side streets to work today? We don't know. Should we eat Grape-Nuts or Corn Flakes for breakfast? Grape-Nuts. (I'm pretty sure about that.)

Our lives overflow with ambiguity. Even if we knew for sure that *this* person has the perfect personality to be our perfect, lifelong mate, there's no guarantee that a week after our honeymoon, a life-altering head injury won't change her personality completely. In life, *we just don't know.*

Yet lifelong uncertainty does not keep us from decision making. We use tools to mitigate the ambiguity: we date for months (or years) before we marry, we explore multiple houses before taking out a mortgage, and we listen to traffic reports before taking side streets to work.

In listening for God's voice, we likewise use tools for discernment. And the first tool is simple: if any word conflicts with God's Word (or to the degree that it conflicts), it isn't a word from God. This is true no matter how strongly we feel, sense, or wish for the word to be true. Of that we *can* be certain.

There are other tools for discernment as well. Such tools cannot replace the definitiveness of the Scripture guidelines, but the Bible itself commends them, and they work together with Scripture to help us sort out God's voice from all the other voices. An indispensable one lies in community discernment of fellow believers.

Find Discernment in Community

When I heard God ask me to leave the mission field, I was young and single, with no debt or attachments. I prayed, asked a few friends for input, and quickly made a decision. I felt I had heard God. Twenty-five years later, when I heard God ask me to leave my software company, I was married with four kids (whom I wanted to send to college), I had a mortgage and a car loan, and the economy was entering a recession. I was less hasty to make a decision.

I asked five men if they would help me discern that word. They met with me twice a month for almost a year. Our community life included these elements:

I looked for a wide range of opinions: I deliberately chose men with differing inclinations. One was pro-charismatic and one anti-charismatic; one was a business executive and one was a pastor; one ran a large nonprofit and one was a professor; and one was my oldest brother (who simply *loves* to give me advice).

I gave the group a hunting license on my life: The group regularly grilled me. They asked me for my life story, what my wife thought of the "word," and how I would extricate myself from the business. They asked me to describe how the word came to me, what the actual words were, and how the sense of that word felt compared to other words I had heard over my lifetime.

We offered the word back to God: We took hours asking for guidance, seeking God's wisdom, examining hidden motivations of my heart that might obscure God's word, and looking for areas in which I might need to repent.

By the end of those months, we unanimously felt a high level of confidence in the word, so I quit my company. Did we know for certain that we had heard accurately? No. But together we lessened the uncertainty.

Get Confirmation

When I was learning to hear a word for someone else (see chapter 8), I was extremely cautious. Aware that something in me wanted the glory of speaking God's word to someone else, I doubted almost every word that came my way. Once, though, I thought God wanted me to tell a young man in my small group that God loved him. It was a simple word, and it agreed with Scripture. But I was nervous.

Then over the next two weeks,

Someone shared at a prayer meeting, "Even the hairs of your head are numbered by God. . . . You are of more value than many sparrows."

I read in Scripture, "It was not because you were greater than other people that the Lord loved you and chose you . . . but it is simply because the Lord loves you."

My father preached a sermon on the love of God.

I even kept hearing the Beatles song "All You Need Is Love" on the radio.

If Scripture, my father, and the Beatles all agreed, I figured there must *certainly* be some truth in it. So I finally shared that simple word with the young man. To this day, I think it was God's word for him. I can't know for sure, but multiple confirmations reduced the uncertainty.

When God is speaking to us, he usually whispers. But it's normally a persistent whisper. When you sense a word from God on your heart, increase your awareness of his multiple confirming repetitions. God will often—I believe usually—confirm his word through Scripture passages, spiritual books, friends, sermons you hear, and external circumstances. Sometimes even the Beatles.

The old Pentecostal confirmation trio was "words, people, and circumstances." There is wisdom in seeing God corroborate his word through the world around us. Even Peter needed the sheet lowered from heaven three times before he believed in its message (Act 10:9–16).

Expect Periodic Conviction of Sin and Idolatry

Years ago I read an article written by a counselor who worked with concentration camp victims shortly after World War II. The sheer breadth of the war's destruction restricted the Allies' ability to help feed and shelter people, so refugee camps were built for the victims.

The counselor noted that many of the victims in the refugee camps acted as though they were still in prison. While they had been freed from the concentration camps, they asked permission for the smallest liberties, such as a nighttime stroll outside their dormitories. The therapist concluded the article with this: "We took the victims out of the camps in an instant, but it may take decades before the camps are taken out of the victims."[1]

That story is just as true about believers. We've been set free, and yet we still live lives that are self-centered, anxious, envious, irritable, and prideful. We've been taken out of prison, but we need God to continually take the prison out of us.

God wants inner freedom for us, but that means he often must convict us of our self-righteous disparagement of our neighbors or our inability to ever accept blame in our fights with our spouse.

Nobody wants to hear this, and I'm not particularly thrilled to write it, but if God's words to us do not include frequent and precise conviction of sins, we must question whether we have learned to recognize God's voice. Read any part of the Scriptures—the narratives, poetry, prophetic books, gospels, or letters—and you'll see that they all shine light on harmful ways that we behave.

> If God's words to us do not include frequent and precise conviction of sins, we must question whether we have learned to recognize God's voice.

If the Bible constantly convicts us of ill behavior, wrong beliefs, and idolatry, then conviction has to be a pattern in all of God's words to us. As Oswald Chambers wrote, "To say that 'prayer changes things' is not as close to the truth as saying, 'Prayer changes *me*.' . . . Prayer is not a matter of changing things externally, but one of working miracles in a person's inner nature."[2]

Learn to Recognize the Sound of God's Voice

Jesus said, "My sheep hear my voice, but they do not know the voice of strangers" (John 10:1–16, 27 SWP). There is a tone to the voice of God that we come to recognize. God speaks words of comfort and affirmation, but it's not flattery; he convicts us of sin but he doesn't condemn; he arouses godly grief that leads to changed hearts, not hopeless grief that leads to death.

There is a quality in the voice of God that differs from the murmurs of the world or our fleshly thoughts or Satan's temptations. As E. Stanley

Jones said, "The voice of the subconscious argues with you, tries to convince you; but the inner voice of God does not argue, does not try to convince you. It just speaks, and it is self-authenticating. It has the feel of the voice of God within it."[3]

There is a feel to the voice of God that we learn to recognize. It simply takes time and experience. The more we hear his voice, the more we recognize it; the more we look for it, the more we find it. Like a mother who recognizes her child's cry in the nursery, we come to recognize the sound, tone, timbre, and messages of God.

Reflect on Past Experiences

During my third year in college, I felt God call me to spend a summer living on a kibbutz (a kind of commune) in Israel. Some friends agreed and others thought it unwise. Though my counsel lacked clarity, I finally decided to go. After returning from my summer abroad, I talked again with all my friends. We reflected on what God had taught me and how the travel gears were greased, and we unanimously agreed: I had heard God's voice.

Sometimes we simply have to act. Then later, we review our decision, preferably with friends. When we do, let's remember the word, the sense of its resonance in our heart, and the sound of the voice we heard. That way, we can know whether to obey it again in the future.

When I worked at my software company, I flew my own small plane to visit clients. After leaving work, I sold the plane. A few years later, I felt a nudge to buy another plane so I could visit men I met on retreats. Some friends thought it was a good idea, and others were unsure. I bought a plane, and that plane was a nightmare until I sold it. When I later reviewed my decision, I think the still, small voice I heard was the whisper of my fleshly desires.

We're not always right. But we can always learn. The tools I have described for confirming God's word don't offer precise guarantees (except to the degree they conform to Scripture). Hearing God's voice is more art than science. I have obeyed senses from God that seemed barren for years before bearing any fruit; had I reviewed (and rejected) them too early, I would have considered them a mistake. Yet I have also "obeyed" what, in honest retrospect, were just fleshly desires. The good news is that God works all things out for the good—sometimes even our mistaken sense of hearing God.

In all words, our trust must be in God, not in our own abilities, gifts, wisdom, or even discernment.

Peace Has Its Role

Yeah, yeah—earlier I said that inner peace isn't a key indicator. But there is a kind of peace that evades us when we fail to obey God's voice. God's word brings disturbance, but ignoring it also brings disturbance of another kind. I didn't want to go on the retreat, but I couldn't sleep until I decided to attend.

Just as God hounded Jonah until he finally obeyed, there is a disturbing lack of peace that hounds us when we disobey or disregard God's word.

When we finally do listen and obey, we get an inner sense that our obedience is right. It's not exactly inner tranquility; it's more like the peace in the eye of a storm: there may be disturbance behind us, and there will likely be difficulties ahead, but in this moment of obedience, we can see clearly.

And in that moment of peace, in the middle of the storm's eye, I grab a box of Grape-Nuts.

Chapter 13

Friendship with the Real God

To follow the imagination of one's heart in the realm of theology is the
way to remain ignorant of God, and to become an idol-worshipper—
the idol in this case being a false mental image of God, made by
one's own speculation and imagination.

—J. I. Packer

There is an incomparable distance between the things which the
imperfect imagine and those which enlightened men
contemplate through revelation from above.

—Thomas à Kempis

Early in 2006, I heard God tell me to leave my software company and to
begin serving him another way. (At least, I *thought* I heard God.) But I
was unsure what that "other way" was. I spent a year attempting to discern it with a few close friends and another year training my replacement.

On January 1, 2008, after decades of secular work, I woke up, took a
shower, poured myself a cup of coffee, and found myself jobless, directionless, and planless.

I was unsure what God had in mind. I had a bunch of ideas, and various people offered numerous suggestions, but I didn't *know* what God
wanted. And he didn't seem to speak anymore. His call to leave a comfortable job had been resounding, but then he seemed to go silent.

Lacking direction and feeling frustrated with the absence of God's
answers, I signed up for a retreat on Calling. Maybe it would help me
gain some clarity on God's purpose for my life.

I rarely talk to passengers on planes, and I *never* introduce myself to speakers at retreats. But I was desperate. My aimless, monotonous morning coffee was growing stale. So I introduced myself to the speaker and asked him if we could talk. We agreed to meet the next month in Colorado. I finally had a plan. Of sorts.

Five weeks later, I met for breakfast with Gary Barkalow. Our breakfast meeting turned into morning coffee, coffee spilled over into lunch, and we spent the afternoon on his deck. Just talking. My ninety-minute breakfast lasted nine hours.

I had flown to Colorado prospecting for answers, and I discovered the goldmine of friendship.

Since then, my friendship with Gary has been far richer than the mere guidance that I hoped to hear from him. We talk, brainstorm, share ideas and frustrations, work together on retreats, encourage and critique each other's writing, and laugh and occasionally cry together. (Just don't tell anyone about the crying part.)

That is what hearing God should mean in our lives. Friendship is what it should look like.

The primary purpose of conversing with God is to know him, to become his friend. We need *friendship* with God more than we need the *guidance* we seek. Oswald Chambers describes it this way: "Spiritual lust causes me to demand an answer from God, instead of seeking God Himself. . . . Whenever we insist that God should give us an answer to prayer we are off track. *The purpose of prayer is that we get ahold of God, not of the answer.*"[1]

The primary purpose of prayer—this "dialogue between two persons who love each other"[2]—is to meet the real God. Our other reasons—like seeking his guidance or assurance—are actually dependent on knowing God personally. Our greatest need is conversational friendship.

False Ideas About God Get in the Way

Sin entered into humanity through a belief—a *mistaken* belief—about God. Satan told Adam and Eve that God had forbidden the fruit because the fruit would dramatically enrich their lives, and God didn't want that. In other words, Satan said that God didn't want the best for them, that he was holding back.

The essence of Satan's message was a lie about who God is.

Humanity's belief in the serpent's lie opened a Pandora's box of hell on earth. All the offspring of sin—oppression, bigotry, rape, loneliness, greed, and despair, among others—entered paradise because of a wrong understanding of the nature of God.

The problems in the world are not caused by *unbelief in* God as much as they are caused by *false beliefs about* God. The greatest troubles in our lives, all our greatest problems, are descendants of our own mistaken beliefs. We don't know the *real* God. A. W. Tozer wrote,

> What comes into the mind when we think of God is the most important thing about us. We tend by a secret law of the soul to move toward our mental image of God.[3]

Each one of us paints mind pictures of God on the canvas of our hearts, and those mental images control our lives. By a "secret law of the soul," our picture of God controls how we raise kids, battle anxiety, seek significance, choose careers, create self-images, and make moral decisions; in short, how we act and feel. We do what we do because of who we believe God to be:

If we imagine God to be busy and distant, then we live in anxiety, fearful that God will fail us in our greatest moment of need.

If we believe God values us little—that we are insignificant to him— we will frantically stockpile all the self-esteem we can amass, often at a cost to others.

If we picture God as a strict schoolmaster, we will work very, very hard, but mostly to avoid him and his criticisms.

If we believe God to be a syrupy-sweet Santa Claus, we will ignore him (though perhaps we'll leave out cookies and milk on Christmas Eve).

Our false mental images of God not only govern our choices, but they also determine our emotional well-being: a harsh God makes us feel condemned and an indifferent God makes us feel abandoned. Even worse, our imaginative images obscure the real God when he appears to us. We fail to see him because he fails to conform to our mental pictures. We humans have always been blinded in this manner, clinging to our forgeries rather than recognizing the real God when he arrives:

- The Pharisees missed God when he healed on the Sabbath.
- The Jewish zealots rejected God because he didn't kick out the Romans.
- Mary Magdalene thought Jesus was a gardener because his body wasn't in the tomb.
- The disciples on the road to Emmaus didn't recognize Jesus because his resurrected body was too ordinary. Where were the fireworks?

It is the same for you and me. We miss God's mighty actions in our lives—we are blind to Jesus walking right next to us—because he doesn't act as we imagine he should. He's there, but we don't see him. Our counterfeit images cloak his presence.

When the poet W. H. Auden became a Christian, his secular friends demanded to know why he converted. His paradoxical answer was, "I believe because [Jesus] fulfills none of my dreams, *because he is in every respect the opposite of what he would be if I could have made him in my own image.*"[4]

To know the real God, we have to let go of our false pictures.

Pursue *Relational* Knowledge

To the Hebrew people of the Old Testament, understanding of truth meant more than an intellectual assent to an abstract idea. Truth was experienced as much as it was articulated; truth was an encounter as much as it was a proposition. To *know* meant a life-changing union, not just a fact-gathering Easter-egg hunt.

Real knowledge is not something one owns like a set of fine china, and spiritual insight is more than a mere assemblage of facts that one collects like baseball cards. Relational knowledge of God—true spiritual wisdom—is a living, breathing, personal power; a voice and a conscience; a movement in the heart; a new pair of eyes and a new way of thinking. It's always an experience.

In seeking to hear God, we are seeking to know him—not just to know *about* God but to meet him and know him as he really is. Seeking to hear God means we are

> In seeking to hear God, we are seeking to know him . . . that is, to spiritually perceive who he is, and his ways and activities in the midst of our daily lives.

seeking to *see* him—that is, to spiritually perceive who he is, and his ways and activities in the midst of our daily lives. This experiential knowledge changes how we view everything. C. S. Lewis said it this way: "I believe in Christianity as I believe that the sun has risen, not only because I see it, but because by it I see everything else."[5]

Seeing God Results in Seeing Ourselves

The very first time I heard God, his word to me was simple: "Sam, I am real, and you don't understand." Perhaps every significant word from God since has been a variation of that theme: that God really is *real*; that my understanding of him is limited and slightly perverted; and that my limited, slightly perverted understanding of God is my real problem.

Knowing God personally changes us. An intimate knowledge of the Creator rearranges our perceptions, desires, hopes, ambitions, and moralities; it is a visit to the eye doctor for vision correction of the eyes of our hearts.

When C. S. Lewis read Tozer's comments on "the most important thing about us," he responded, "I read in a periodical the other day that the fundamental thing is how we think of God. By God Himself, it is not! How God thinks of us is not only more important, but infinitely more important."[6] Elsewhere he wrote, "What are we to make of Jesus Christ? This is a question which has, in a sense, a frantically comic side. For the real question is not what are we to make of Christ, but what is He to make of us?"[7]

Every time God speaks to us, we also get a glimpse of ourselves. And we often dislike what we see. The friends of W. H. Auden persisted in asking him, *Why Jesus? Why not Socrates, Buddha, Confucius, or Mohammed?* He answered them with bone-chilling honesty, "None of the others arouse all sides of my being to cry, 'Crucify Him.'"[8]

> Every time God speaks to us, we also get a glimpse of ourselves.

We seek God with the hopes of experiencing some sunlit plain or starry night; we look for peace and comfort. In my experience of God, though, he almost always *afflicts my comfort before comforting my affliction.*[9] Jesus promises that the pure in heart shall see God (Matt. 5:8), and God's purifying my heart often requires the affliction of his gentle surgery on a tumor in my heart. But the surgery always results in the comfort of a heart made free.

What we need from God, and what he provides, is *true* comfort, not merely a "There, there, it's all right." He offers a heart-arresting, and then heart-resurrecting, vision of his undeserved, unmerited, and unbelievable love. And we can begin to see—to really *see*—God in Scripture.

How Can We Come to Know God in Scripture?

For most of my secular friends, the four biggest problems with Scripture are these:

1. Its historicity ("It was written too late. Who knows what the real Jesus was like?")
2. Its miracles ("How can a modern person believe in the virgin birth?")
3. Its exclusivity ("What do you mean, Jesus is the *only* way?")
4. Its culture ("How can you believe in a wrathful God, and sin, and bloody sacrifices?")

For most of my Christian friends, those issues aren't obstacles. They either know reasonable answers or trust in God's goodness for what they don't understand. Their biggest problem with Scripture is that it doesn't seem real. We read the narratives and prophecies as though they are epic stories like The Lord of the Rings—powerful legends, sure, but they don't seem real. We believe them to be true, but the customs, language, and miracles feel alien to twenty-first-century culture. What do the clay tablets of the Ten Commandments have to do with the electronic instant-messaging of Facebook? Sometimes even The Lord of the Rings seems more real.

Our problem is how to see the reality of God in the reality of Scripture. We see the world and we know it's real; we need to see God with the same sense of realness. Years ago, Norman Grubb wrote,

> We fail to bridge the gap within us between God's thoughts and God's word of faith because we are bound by the domination of the visible. We see the blind eye, the withered arm: Christ saw . . . the power of His Father to heal, and spoke the word. "Stretch forth thine arm," "Receive thy sight." We see the five loaves and the multitudes, and say, "What are they among so many?" Christ saw His Father's . . . unlimited supply . . . [and] acted on the full assurance of it.[10]

Hearing God involves an inner engagement in which truth becomes real. And all deep knowledge of God—and thus hearing from him—begins with meeting the real God in Scripture. Here are some suggestions for helping Scripture come alive.

Ask God to make it happen. Scripture says that we don't have because we don't ask or because we ask for the sake of selfish pleasures (James 4:2–3). Asking God to make Scripture come alive for us is a prayer we know God wants to grant.

Ask God to reveal himself through his mysteries. Spiritual mysteries are different from modern mysteries. In modern mysteries, we assemble clues and solve the riddle. Biblical mysteries cannot be figured out; they can only be revealed. The ultimate mystery is God himself, so let's ask God to reveal himself in the seemingly paradoxical mysteries of his Word.

Ask, "How would I have acted?" Biblical narratives become real when they engage us. Jesus was always surprising people; let him surprise you too.

Place yourself in the shoes of any character in any biblical story and ask yourself what you would have done. When the law expert asks Jesus what he needs to do to be saved, stop and ask how you would have answered, and then read what Jesus said (Mark 10:17–31).

Ask, "What would I have thought?" Whenever you read a command in Scripture, ask yourself how it differs from your own wisdom on the subject. Be ruthlessly honest with your answers. Say your "Sigh-oxes" out loud and let God unveil your false beliefs so you can see aright. When God restricts sexual behaviors, what is your reaction? When Jesus speaks harshly to the Pharisees, how do you respond to his seeming callousness? Let God's wisdom shock your own.

Picture the scene in your mind. As you read, take the details described and try to picture the event. Think of what it would be like to have a lame man lowered down from the ceiling. Picture a crowd of people wanting to stone a woman while Jesus doodles in the dust. As you read the prophets, imagine their admonition against *your* idolatry and injustice.

Look for seeming inconsistencies. The wisdom of God is beyond us and sometimes confuses us. Seek God in those curiosities. In 1 Corinthians, Paul says we should "not pronounce judgment before the time, before the Lord comes" (1 Cor. 4:5); but then Paul says he has "already pronounced judgment" on a person who had given himself over to a sinful choice (1 Cor. 5:3); and later yet he says that "the saints will judge the world" (1 Cor. 6:2). Take these passages to God and ask him to reveal himself through them.

Ask how your life can be different. As you read a story, letter, psalm, or prophecy, consider how your life could be different if you believed what that Scripture reveals about God's nature. For instance, when you see God showing himself faithful to people who frequently fail him, such as Abraham, David, and the disciples, ask yourself how much more peaceful you'd be if you personally knew this God of faithfulness.

Pray, "Let me know you and be known by you." Express to God your desire to know him personally, and tell him that you long to be known by him.

Hudson Taylor was a missionary to China who changed forever the way missions operate. He had that impact because he himself was changed, and he was changed because he saw God. Every morning he began his day with these words: "Lord Jesus make Thyself to me, a living, bright Reality."[11]

In that same living, bright reality that Taylor knew, we too will find the Friend we've always wanted to meet, whom we long to see, and who invites us, "Walk with me."

Chapter 14

Emotions and Experiences of God

*There is a difference between having an opinion that
God is holy and gracious, and having a sense of the
loveliness and beauty of that holiness and grace.*
—Jonathan Edwards

*For the Word of God is not received by faith if it flits about in the top
of the brain, but [only] when it takes root in the depth of the heart.*
—John Calvin

When I was fourteen years old, I had an awe-inspiring experience of God. It happened during a small prayer meeting with twenty other teenagers, all sitting in a circle. While singing a song, something began to stir in me. Soon I sensed a nerve-jingling, spine-tingling, tangible presence of God.

I experienced physical tremors; every nerve seemed electrified, hyper-alert, and intensely aware. I felt alive and bubbling over, caught up in a kind of euphoria. I sat down because I feared falling down. My body shook as my heart pounded, and I prayed, *"I love you, I love you, I love you."* The experience lasted close to an hour.

Later that evening, I wasn't sure what had happened. But I liked it.

I asked God for more of it. In subsequent weeks and months, in prayer times and in prayer meetings, I'd pray, "Anoint me again; I want *that* again; let me soak in *that* some more." But the sense of exhilaration didn't return—at least, not with the same intensity.

Skip ahead forty years to last week (okay, okay, skip ahead forty-*four* years). I had just returned from a retreat and I was worn out, perhaps a bit crabby. The following morning something similar happened again. I felt stirred and moved; somehow I sensed the reality of God. My prayer time lasted four hours.

But this experience was different. Instead of euphoria, I sensed an inner insight into the *abundance* of God. I felt a thrill, yes, but it didn't come directly from stirred emotions. No tingling of the spine. Rather, it was a *response* to my perception of the fullness and weightiness of God. I saw God in my mind.

It began as I read the classic devotional *My Utmost for His Highest*, followed by a familiar verse from the gospel of John. Every word seemed to pulsate. It was like the difference between reading a menu and tasting the meal. The words were the same as I'd read before, but they were more vibrant, as though animated, or touchable, or tasteable:

> And this is eternal life: to know you, the only true God, and to know the one whom you sent—Jesus the Messiah. (John 17:3 SWP)

The *familiarity* of the verse faded away in the *freshness* of tasting the words. They were more than typed words on a printed page. I heard the voice of God illuminating its Speaker. I wasn't reading something about God; I was *meeting* God. Eternal life became more than a mathematical extension of mere existence; it became a corporeal connection with the personhood of God.

Be Wary of "Experiences"

I've never been opposed to "experiences" of God. I've liked the sensations when they happened to me. But I've been a bit wary of them. I've seen too many people (including me) pursue God primarily for feelings. Yet those feelings seem transitory and non-transforming: today we experience euphoria in prayer, but tomorrow our work supervisor still scares us to death.

I used to have a friend who described himself as a "recovering charismatic." He was open to "the gifts," but his experience of many charismatics made him leery. He grew up in a home where his mother frenetically flitted from one worship experience to the next. First it was the "Toronto Blessing" of the mid-1990s; then it was the revival in Brownsville, Florida; then Bethel Church; and then anywhere she heard that something was happening.

Worship music blared interminably throughout the house. She seemed to need its euphoric oomph to motivate her for the tiniest of tasks. Wiping kitchen counters took the combined efforts of Matt Redman, Chris Tomlin, and Paul Baloche.

Don't ask what spring cleaning required.

Despite her repeated worship experiences, my friend said his mother remained stuck in her anxiety, anger, and self-concern. She would say, "I just want to go where God is working," but to my friend it seemed that she just wanted to go wherever there was an escape from everyday life, a place where she could have her problems sedated.

I don't know how unfair my friend's childhood memories are; I never met his mother, and I don't know what traumas she might have been trying to numb. But I've known that same ceaseless quest for ecstatic excitement.

What Do We Really Need?

We need inner changes. Anxiety, stress, and confusion often overwhelm us. It's great to experience an inner exhilaration that dulls our pain, but it's better to have an inner transformation that displaces the pain's roots.

Many words have multiple meanings. When we accidentally mix those meanings, our understanding gets hijacked. "Feeling" is one of those tricky words. We usually equate feeling with emotions, but it has multiple other meanings as well:

When I feel a toothache, I refer to physical pain.
When I feel I took a wrong turn, I mean a mental impression.
When I feel for the light switch, I describe my sense of touch.
When I feel like a Coke, I voice a desire.
And when I feel sad, I express an emotion.

There's one more important meaning for feeling: *belief*. If a friends says she "feels unimportant," she means she *believes* she is unimportant (or that others consider her to be unimportant). Beliefs always and simultaneously determine emotions. That's why we confuse the two. If your friend "feels" unimportant, she will immediately "feel" sad as well. Her belief of insignificance triggers her emotion of sadness.

Beliefs and emotions are cause and effect, so they are hard to separate. But they are different. If we only address our emotions and not the beliefs that cause them, we're taking aspirin for an abscessed tooth and skipping the dentist's chair. We are going to hurt just the same tomorrow.

> It's great to experience an inner exhilaration that dulls our pain, but it's better to have an inner transformation that displaces the pain's roots.

Our desire to feel good—or at least to stop feeling bad—makes us want to short-circuit the surgery and jump to the good feelings. We feel sad (or scared, or ashamed), and we want to end that pain, so we visit the bar for a bottle or travel to Macy's for a new outfit. But our deep belief (*my life is a failure, I'm unattractive, I'm unimportant, nobody cares*) has not been dealt with. So tomorrow we're back to the bottle for comfort or to Macy's for matching shoes.

In my pursuit of "one more" experience of God, I had sipped from the same bottle; I tried to short-circuit my inner wiring. I went straight for the ecstasy. In my teenage euphoric experience, my spirit sensed the reality of God, and my resultant response was nerve-electrifying joy. But afterward, instead of looking for a deeper comprehension of the *reality* of God (with its resultant belief that triggers joy), I searched for more nerve-tingling feelings—more shaking and quaking.

We Need Encounters with God

Blaise Pascal was a seventeenth-century child-prodigy mathematician, physicist, and philosopher. In 1654 he had an experience of God that completely changed his life. He wrote about it on a small note that

he sewed into his coat lining. It was unknown until a servant accidentally discovered it after his death. The note said,

> In the year 1654, Monday 23 November . . . from half-past ten in
> the evening to half-past midnight. Fire.
>   The God of Abraham, the God of Isaac, the God of Jacob. Not
> of the philosophers and intellectuals. Certitude, certitude, feel-
> ing, joy, peace. The God of Jesus Christ. My God and your God.
>   Joy, joy, joy, tears of joy. My God . . . May I not be separated
> from him eternally.[1]

Pascal experienced a taste of the living God, not the abstract menu-
god of the philosophers (and remember, Pascal *was* a philosopher).
Something in his experience changed his entire belief system about
Jesus: God became real. Pascal met the eternal, living Lord who had also
been the God of Abraham, Isaac, and Jacob. The experience was fire in
Pascal's soul.

His experience gave him a "certitude," an assured confidence, a belief
that moved beyond his head to grip his heart. His resultant emotion was
"joy, tears of joy."

When I heard God in my bedroom say to the ten-year-old me, "Sam,
I am real, and you don't understand," I too first experienced a certitude.
All my watered-down, insubstantial reasons for disbelief instantly
evaporated in the cauldron of meeting God. I didn't sense joy as much
as a fire that God was real and that knowing him was all I would ever
need. It was an electric peace, a pulsating certainty. It restructured my
inner life.

In the nineteenth century, Dwight L. Moody (a prominent Chicago
pastor) stopped in New York on his way to Europe. Strolling down Wall
Street, he experienced God. He later wrote,

> One day in the city of New York—oh, what a day!—I can-
> not describe it, I seldom refer to it . . . I can only say that God
> revealed Himself to me, and I had such an experience of His
> love that I had to ask Him to stay His hand.[2]

We need experiences of God. The experiences we need, however, are not primarily the feeling of *emotion* but feelings of life-changing *belief.* We need God to speak to his Spirit within us, to resonate in our hearts, to move our factual knowledge of God beyond menu reading to tasting the meal. You'll get all the emotions you need (or can handle) after that belief-busting heart change of meeting the real God.

We need that inner change of heart. We are too easily filled with fear, shame, and anger. Emotional euphoria may anesthetize our worries, but only a heart-stopping, then defibrillating encounter with the reality of God can remove them.

Eternal life is knowing God. It's not merely possessing knowledge *about* him, or "being good" in the way we behave, or experiencing a rush of emotions. God has made it possible for us to actually know, converse with, and even experience *him.* That is the real answer for life.

Emotions are not the deepest part of us; however, they reveal our deepest beliefs. And those beliefs can be changed and renewed only through God's revelation of himself.

Should We Ask God for an Experience?

Our inner being seeks, thirsts, pants, even faints for God (Ps. 42: 1–2). We can't help it. It's written on the DNA of our hearts. It's an inner tidal wave of our spirit. Do I want another spine-tingling, euphoric experience of God? Sure, bring it on! Even more, though, I need the spine-*strengthening* inner knowledge of his reality—his self-revelation—to change my deepest beliefs.

To hear God is to come to know God, and to know God is to begin to hear him.

Knowing God is our goal in hearing him. We think we need comfort or direction, but the only comfort and direction we need is seeing God. The patriarch Job never got answers to his questions—he got God. The psalmist in Psalm 73 saw the success of evil men and despaired—until he saw God. The writer of Hebrews saw the world rebelling against God and said our solution is, "We see him" (Heb. 2.9).

It is perfectly consistent with Scripture to ask to see—to hear and know—God. With the psalmist, we can pray,

God, you are my God! I eagerly seek you. My soul thirsts for you
and my flesh faints for you as in a dry, weary, and parched land.
(Ps. 63:1 SWP)

Paul spends much of chapter 3 in Ephesians praying that we would
experience God. He asks

first: that we be "strengthened with power through [God's] Spirit in
[our] inner being" (v. 16);
then: that we have the "strength to comprehend" God's love (v. 18;
the Greek word for "comprehend" means "to be seized" as a city is
seized by a conquering general, so Paul prays that we be overcome
by God's love);
finally: that we know "the width, length, height, and depth of the love
of Christ, and that we know something that goes beyond knowledge" (vv. 18–19 SWP).

Paul is praying for an inner, God-given certainty of Christ's love, a
knowledge that surpasses knowledge. Paul is praying for an *experience*—
an experience of knowing God (and his love for us) with such certainty
that our lives explode in joy.

If the psalmists and Paul can ask this of God, then it's perfectly fine
for us to seek it as well. If we only aim for euphoria, we'll eventually
experience emptiness. But if we aim for God, we'll get everything else we
ever wanted thrown in.

Chapter 15

God Speaks in Our Detours

Earth's crammed with Heaven, and every common bush
afire with God; but only he who sees takes off his shoes.
—Elizabeth Barrett Browning

Years ago, a business client asked me to speak at an industry conference. Our company encouraged employees to speak at these events. Their presentations showcased the expertise of our employees and gave the company a bit of prestige. So being asked wasn't new, though my prior engagements had been limited to leading breakout sessions on arcane business issues with fifteen or twenty participants.

This time the client asked me to speak on the topic of CRM. I had never heard the acronym before, but acronyms like hummingbirds flit in and out of business lingo all the time. My ignorance didn't concern me. I jotted down the date in my Day-Timer and then forgot about it.

The day before the conference, the client phoned to express his enthusiasm for my upcoming presentation. He was curious about what perspective I would offer. He said, "I've never seen you give a keynote presentation before."

An icy fist gripped my intestines and squeezed. *I hadn't known I was the keynote speaker.* I had figured it would just be another small, boring sideshow. Now I pictured scores of eager experts staring with wide-eyed wonder at my abysmal ignorance. I imagined tomatoes thrown, boos hurled, and unbearable humiliation.

I still didn't know what CRM even meant. *How could I have been so stupid?*

In dismay, I googled "CRM," printed out the first five articles, and then dashed off to the airport. If you've ever experienced professional panic, multiply it by ten and you'll sense the faintest hint of my terror. I was going to flop. The flippancy in my preparation would reveal itself in front of a crowd of experts. I was a fraud, and the CRM world (whatever that was) would soon know it.

I parked my car, boarded the plane, and sat in my assigned seat. I'm an introvert and rarely disturb the passenger next to me on an airplane; they sit quietly and I sit silently. Like it should be.

But this time, my nervous energy needed an outlet. So I talked, and discovered that my seatmate happened to hold the chair of public speaking at an Ivy League college. He smiled friendly-like, so I casually said, "I'm speaking tomorrow at a conference. Would you mind giving me some tips for good public speaking?"

"It's actually quite easy," he replied. "The number one rule for good public speaking is, 'Know what you're talking about.'"

The icy grip squeezed tighter. After an awkward pause, I asked, "What's rule number two?"

"The second rule for great presentations is just as easy: 'Love what you're talking about.'"

Strike two. Undoubtedly knowledge and passion are great starting points—provided you in fact know and love your topic. But his expertise only exacerbated my fears.

I asked if he had any remaining advice, like an idea for an opening joke, or good graphics, or audience involvement. He paused, perhaps sensing my anxiety, and then said, "When Winston Churchill became prime minister of Britain at the beginning of World War II, he gave a radio address. In it he said, 'I feel like my whole life has prepared me for this moment.'"[1]

"Sam," he continued, "the best advice I can give you is to recognize that your entire life has prepared you for this moment, for this one presentation."

It was the best advice I've ever heard for public speaking. But again it failed to address my current predicament. Instead, it did something better—and scarier: it sent a shock wave coursing through me that was even more terrifying than my upcoming humiliation.

What was *my whole life about?*

What was I doing, bouncing around from conference to conference, assignment to assignment, day after day? Where was I going?

I had no idea what my life had prepared me for. Suddenly I felt lost, adrift, aimless, and scared.

God Shouts to Wake Us Up

Most of our life progresses step by step, day by day, and is built stone by stone. Birthdays come and go. Our children exchange diapers for training pants, and soon they move from first grade to second. On the way to work we get a flat tire, and then at work we receive a pay raise. Life goes on, moment after moment, and it's mostly a picture of routine.

We're like truckers driving one mile after another. Most of our journey is unremarkable. But every once in a while, a major roadblock disrupts our travel: we get laid off from work, a child is born with autism, or we discover that we really hate our chosen career. While God's normal voice is quiet, in these times we find a different timbre. "God whispers to us in our pleasures, speaks in our conscience, but shouts in our pains: it is His megaphone to rouse a deaf world."[2]

I believe that a daily, quiet, conversational relationship—a walk with God—is meant to be the foundation of our lives. But there are occasions when our travels need disruption. Our routine has lulled us to sleep, our rivers of life have become stagnant pools of despair. God needs to wake us up for the next stage in our journey. It is time for a major realignment.

God speaks to us in the detours of our lives.

Moses spent forty years training in Pharaoh's court, and he spent another forty training in the deserts of Midian. Then one routine, boring day on the job, he saw something inexplicable: a bush on fire that wasn't consumed by the flames. It made no sense. He said to himself, "I will turn aside to see this great sight, why the bush is not burned" (Exod. 3:3).

Our tendency—at least my tendency—is to react to a baffling circumstance by making a plan. If I'm laid off, I rewrite my résumé. That's being responsible, and responsibility is wise. But it's not *all*-wise. Sometimes we must turn aside to examine the mystery unfolding before us. *What is God up to?*

The Hebrew word for "turn aside" can be translated "detour." Moses decided that the mystery he witnessed deserved a detour from his daily routine. God allows disruptions in our lives, anomalies that make no sense, to wake us up. He invites us to take a detour.

By all means, rewrite your résumé, take your child to a specialist, or take whatever action is needed for your situation. But also recognize that this moment—this perplexing, mystifying moment—is an invitation from God to take a detour. God has something significant to say, but we've been hypnotized by our monotonous routines. Our humdrum lives obscure his words. He needs to wake us up. Sometimes God needs to shout in our pain.

> God allows disruptions in our lives, anomalies that make no sense, to wake us up.

God Has Prepared Us for This

It turned out that CRM stands for Customer Relationship Management (at least in my industry), and our software did CRM very well. I was even part of the team that designed its functionality into our software package. So I did in fact know CRM well; I even loved it to some degree. My coworkers and I were CRM innovators, and God had indeed prepared me my whole life—at least, my whole software life—for this moment. My company just called our expertise by a different name.

God has been preparing each one of us our entire lives for this moment—the moment you are in right now—but we often fail to recognize his preparation because we've given his training a different name.

I gave a decent speech, no one threw tomatoes, and my impending mortification evaporated. But Churchill's words, shared with me by a fellow passenger in a seemingly chance conversation, began to haunt me. My own speech was soon history, the sponsoring company eventually went out of business (doubtless for hiring questionable speakers like me), and I have forgotten almost everything I said that evening.

But the stranger's words plagued me. An inner resonance told me that God was speaking something weighty in this moment. I couldn't shake the sense that God wanted more for my life.

Decades before, I had wanted to "speak God's word" to God's people.

Those longings were now faint memories. A casual conversation with a stranger on a plane reawakened all those old dreams. *What was I doing with my life?*

Over the next several years, I began to turn aside. I took periodic detours to examine my own burning bush: the unsettling anomaly of an outwardly successful life that was so easily terrorized by a sense of pointlessness.

I soon experienced a growing dissatisfaction with my job. I was an executive and owner of a highly successful software company, I made more money than I had ever imagined, and I was respected in the industry. These outward trappings had a grip on my life.

But over time, in detour after detour, their hold on me loosened.

When I finally heard God tell me to leave my job for something new, I was ready. Once again, God had prepared my life for that moment, though my name for my situation was different from his. I thought I was disillusioned with work. God called it reawakening his dream.

Take the Detours

God invites us to walk with him in the detours of our lives. But detour moments, like our cell phones, have a wide assortment of ringtones. If we fail to recognize an enigmatic life event as God's rousing us from sleep, we will miss his invitation to turn aside.

I'm aware of four detour signs found in Scripture that help us discern God's wake-up call in our own lives.

The Invitation of Scientific Anomalies

These are the times when a challenge confronts our normal understanding of the physical rules. We call these events *miracles*. Our normal response to them (apart from disbelief) is wonder and amazement; however, I believe God wants more. He wants a reorientation in our hearts to a deeper reality. Inevitably, the miracles of God lead us to a realignment in our thinking.

Moses and the burning bush. God called Moses to more than mere wonder; he called him to a career change and a heretofore-hidden boldness.

Water and manna in the wilderness. In supplying the Israelites with life-giving water and food, God foreshadowed a coming, deeper source of life in his Son. When Jesus shockingly said, "Eat my body and drink my blood," he was connecting God's miracles of sustenance to himself, taking us down a reorienting detour to reveal that the person of God is all that will satisfy our inner being.

Jesus walking on the water. Every other miracle of Jesus simply restored God's original, natural order: God's plan didn't include hunger, blindness, or death. Jesus's naked display of mastery over the elements makes a powerful point: it means that everything is under God's control, from the waves of the sea to the storms of our lives.

The Invitation of Theological Oddities

If God's ways are not our ways, then we should expect challenges to our understanding of his ways. The very first time I heard God, my ten-year-old, shallow theology had just been rocked. I expected God to bless non-cussers (like me) by making them "cool." God's theological oddity of acting in ways that shocked me also led to my first experience of hearing God.

When something doesn't make sense to us theologically, when all we've sensed to date seems shaken, then is a great time to take a detour. God won't create a new theology for us, but he will teach us something that will shake us.

Jonah's call to Nineveh. God called Jonah to speak a word of repentance to Israel's hostile pagan neighbors. This made no sense to Jonah. He didn't want those unwashed Ninevites to experience the blessing of repentance; he hated the idea of God's mercy for those heathen. The book of Jonah is about God speaking to Jonah about his own racist heart.

Job's distress. Job judged himself highly righteous, and his miserable counselors judged him to be a secret hypocrite because God blesses the good and curses the evil. (Wait, that sounds like my adolescent theology!) But God had a greater purpose in the theological oddity of Job's condition. The book concludes with Job seeing God—and that, Job says, is all he needs.

Peter's call to preach to Cornelius. We typically hear only what we want to hear and tune out the contrary. Throughout Scripture, for instance, God's people are called to serve the nations, but they resist (see Jonah above). Then in the New Testament, God changes Peter's heart with the shocking (to a Jew) vision of an invitation to eat unclean food. It initiated the spread of the gospel to the Gentiles (Acts 10). And I, for one, am glad of it.

The Invitation of Hardships

God speaks to us in our pain. Ask anyone who has been a believer for more than five years and they will reluctantly admit that their greatest growth came in times of deepest trouble. We all know it, and we all hate it.

But there is no other way. We are addicts to poison, and God needs to send us to a detox center for withdrawal. There is no true satisfaction in this world, yet we always turn to the world for satisfaction. Thomas à Kempis asks, "How is it possible to love a life that has such great bitterness, that is subject to so many calamities and miseries . . . [that] begets so many deaths and plagues? And yet, it is loved, and many seek their delight in it."[3]

God must surgically remove the tumors on our hearts that leech away our lifeblood from the only pleasures that will satisfy. And it hurts.

Joseph's many trials. It was in the ordeal of betrayal, false accusation, and imprisonment that God purified Joseph's heart to make him great. Later Joseph summarized his whole life to his brothers with one short sentence: "You meant evil against me, but God meant it for good" (Gen. 50:20).

Paul's thorn in the flesh. Hundreds of doctoral dissertations have been written on the nature of Paul's enigmatic allusion to his physical distress. The truth is, nobody on earth knows what he was talking about. But we do know this: Paul said that when he begged God to remove his suffering, God spoke: "My grace is enough for you; my power is made perfect in weakness" (2 Cor. 12:9 SWP). Even Paul needed a tumor removal.

The Invitation of Disillusionment

Discouragement often accompanies theological peculiarities or the hardships of life (see Job). At times it feels like nothing we do—nothing!—works. Everything implodes, all our great plans nosedive, and every desire for good seems thwarted. *What is God about?*

God is dis-illusioning us; he is exposing and expunging the delusions we hold so fiercely. Like Prince Rilian in C. S. Lewis's *The Silver Chair,* we need a dis-enchantment. We think we are riding high when we are really enslaved to an evil witch, the pleasures of this world.

The psalms are filled with cries of despair and sighs of dereliction. They accompany the triumph of foes, the failure of crops, and weaknesses of the body. They walk hand in hand with the loss of worldly comforts. But there is always a hint of a hope of restoration, that enemies will be beaten and health will return.

There is one disillusionment in Scripture—only one that I know—with no hope of restoration. Of all disillusionments, this may be the harshest: the despair of absolute success.

Solomon's cry of emptiness. Imagine, if you can, having everything your heart desires. Not one thing under the sun is withheld from you—yet you feel empty. There is no hope of a restoration of lost comforts because you have every comfort. Solomon was the richest king and the wisest man, he had more sexual partners than a porn star, and his palaces and gardens were matchless. Yet he wrote Ecclesiastes, the book that says, "All is nothing, a fruitless chasing after the wind" (Eccl. 1:14 SWP). Solomon needed a dis-enchantment.

Very few people in this world reach the pinnacle of their careers, but for those who do, it means the ultimate form of discouragement. Their lives are signposts for all of us. God speaks to us in our pain, in the detours of our lives. Let's listen.

Don't Ignore God's Shout

We live with the familiar. When the unfamiliar arrives—and it will—take a detour with God. Let all the aberrations of this life, from its miracles, to its theological quandaries, to its hardships and discourage-ments, point you to the One who is with you in the fires. He is speaking—shouting, even—in the circumstances that shake your heart.

Let his shaking continue until the only thing that remains is that which cannot be shaken (Heb. 12:27). God speaks in the whispers of peace, but he also speaks in the whirlwinds of struggle (Job 40:6).

How do we take this detour with God? We put into practice all that we've learned so far: we meditate on the Scriptures, we brainstorm with God, we converse with him about our confusion and pain, and we ask friends for their time, counsel, and prayer.

And we wait.

G. Campbell Morgan wrote, "Wherever there are hearts waiting for the Voice of God, that Voice is to be heard."[4]

Chapter 16

Hearing God in the Ordinary

Every single act and feeling, every experience, whether pleasant or
unpleasant, must be referred to God. It means looking at everything as
something that comes from Him, and always looking to Him and asking
His will first, and saying: "How would He wish me to deal with this?"
—C. S. Lewis

Ever since I was a young boy, I wanted to learn to fly. In 1997, after years of wanting but not doing, I began to take flight lessons. The lessons taught me how to take off and land, how to navigate using instruments and charts, and how to communicate with aviation radios.

I particularly liked learning to land.

On my third flight, my instructor, Jayne, pulled the plane's throttle to idle and announced that my engine had just "died." She asked what I was going to do. While throttling her was not an option (because I hadn't yet learned to land), I was strongly tempted. She then taught me a set of procedures to follow, and soon this "engine-out" test became a regular part of my flight training:

- My instructor killed the engine when I didn't expect it.
- I pitched the plane for its ideal glide speed.
- I followed the airplane's engine restart checklist.
- I searched for a safe place to land within gliding distance.
- We would glide down to the potential landing site until Jayne decided whether I could have landed safely or not.
- Then she would rethrottle the engine, and we would review what I had done.

Week after week and month after month, Jayne tested my skills with these engine-out procedures. She drilled them into me so thoroughly that I could have landed an engine-out airplane in my sleep. Though I never tried.

God's Tests Are Instructions

One day, as I easily glided my engine-out plane to yet another farmer's field, I realized that Jayne had taught me to fly by taking me through a series of tests. The nature of her tests—repetition followed by reflection—yielded the fruit of aviation instincts. As Jayne and I flew the plane back to altitude (after I "passed" another engine-out test), the spontaneous thought came to me that Jayne's tests of my flying skills reflected God's tests of my life.

I had always pictured the tests of God to be like college entrance exams: *these are the tests that make or break our lives.* If we "pass," we are accepted into prestigious universities; if we "fail," we are rejected. But my image of God's tests was completely wrong. God's tests train us for life exactly as Jayne's tests trained me to pilot an aircraft in an emergency.

Educators call these training tests *formative tests.* They are educational methods that instruct us in the midst of the test, just like my flight instructor's engine-out surprises. Each time Jayne killed the engine, it was a test, and the test trained me to handle emergencies.

Formative tests teach us today how to avoid disqualification (or death!) tomorrow.

However, most of us picture spiritual tests as *summative tests.* Summative tests (such as college entrance exams, midterms, and finals) measure our past learning achievements. One could say that summative tests are designed to *disqualify* us, as in, "My college entrance score was so low, I failed to get into Harvard."

The writer of Hebrews explains, "For the moment all discipline seems painful rather than pleasant, but later *it yields the peaceful fruit of righteousness* to those who have been trained by it" (Heb. 12:11); and James encourages us, "Count it all joy, my brothers, when you meet trials of various kinds, for . . . *the testing of your faith produces steadfastness*" (James 1:2–3).

Both writers tell us that God's tests aren't designed to disqualify us;

quite the opposite. In those ordinary engine-out training moments—ordinary but never dull—God spoke a word to me: that the tests of God are teaching us to fly.

God Speaks in the Commonplace

I share my flight-training story because it illustrates the nature of God's voice in our lives. Most of the time it seems quite ordinary. No lightning, thunder, or mystical feelings. In the middle of my exciting flying experience (every time the engine decelerated to idle, my heart accelerated to full throttle), God's voice came quietly, simply a resonance in my heart, and told me that this is how God trains me.

The voice was so quiet that you might say it was just my own thoughts; however, it revealed to me a bit of the mystery of the gospel. And only God can reveal his mysteries (Eph. 3:3).

During the end of the period of the Judges, the boy Samuel heard God call to him three times in the middle of the night, and three times Samuel mistook the ordinary-sounding voice of God for the voice of his master, Eli. Three times Samuel ran to his master and said, "Here I am." Eli finally figured out that Samuel was hearing the voice of God. He said, "If the voice comes again, reply, 'Speak, Lord, for your servant is listening'" (1 Sam. 3:9 SWP).

God's voice came to Samuel in an unremarkable manner. No trumpets, fires, or lightning. In fact, when Samuel heard the mighty voice of God, he mistook it for the reedy sighs of his aged master. The everyday voice of God is so gentle, it feels so familiar, that we frequently miss it. Or we confuse it with the voice of a friend or the stranger sitting next to us. Psalm 19 begins, "The heavens proclaim the glory of God, and the skies boldly display his craftsmanship. Day after day they gush forth words, and night after night they reveal knowledge. There is neither speech nor words; their voice is not heard. Yet their voice fills all the earth, and their words travel to the ends of the world" (vv. 1–4 SWP).

God fills the earth with his voice. He is speaking to us everywhere, in all moments, though perhaps most often in the commonplace and routine. His voice is not restricted to the awe-inspiring beauty of the sunset; it also is heard in life's everyday activities—mowing the lawn, taking out the trash, driving to the store. Oswald Chambers wrote, "We look for visions from heaven and for earth-shaking events to see God's power. Yet we never realize that all the time God is at work in our everyday events and in the people around us."[1]

> He is speaking to us everywhere, in all moments, though perhaps most often in the commonplace and routine.

The utter *ordinariness* of God's voice distracts us from his messages to us. Day to day and night to night he is speaking. But like Samuel running to Eli, we go to therapists and self-help books, and to them we declare, "Here I am."

We need to heed Eli's counsel and reply to God, "Speak, Lord, for your servant is listening."

Expect to Hear God

Eli's recommendation ("Tell God, 'I'm listening'") implies active participation. The word Eli uses for "listen" means to pay attention, to focus our minds, to purposely put away distractions so we can willfully hear. It means we are engaged, we *involve* ourselves, in the process of hearing God's voice.

If we are alone in our house during the daytime, we may hear all kinds of noises, but the noises are easily ignored. When we are alone in the house at night, however, those same sounds seize our attention. The tick of a clock or the creak of wooden floorboards raises questions in our minds: "Was that a footfall I just heard?"

In like manner, we can heighten our awareness of God's voice by regularly praying, "Speak, Lord, for your servant is listening." And then, of course, we listen. We become aware that God speaks through

the beauty and power of nature
the brilliance and conflicts of colleagues at work
books and movies
highway billboards
the words of a friend
a bicycle ride

and countless other methods and moments, as many as are available to an infinitely imaginative Creator.

In response, something stirs inside us, and we ask, "Is that you, Lord? Are you speaking?" As Oswald Chambers wrote, "If I am united with Jesus Christ, I hear God all the time through the devotion of hearing. A flower, a tree, or a servant of God may convey God's message to me. What hinders me from hearing is my attention to other things."[2]

Hearing God in the ordinary requires loyalty to the expectation that God wants to speak with us. It means we choose to wrest our attention away from obvious, external circumstances and fix it on the message God has for us in the moment. Because he *is* speaking.

I was once asked to become president of a company I worked for, but I didn't feel ready, and I suggested a colleague of mine instead. When my friend became president, he immediately demoted me, publicly humiliated me, and began a campaign to discredit me. I was bewildered by this unexpected onslaught and confused about what to do. I asked God if I should resign, defend myself, or aggressively fight back.

For a couple of months I heard no answer. Finally, while waiting at an airport, I overheard a conversation between two women. One woman mentioned that she had recently sat for several hours in the waiting room of her car mechanic. At the end of her wait, a long-lost friend appeared to pick up her own car. They were able to reconnect after fifteen years of interrupted friendship.

The woman in the airport concluded, "In an instant, that long wait seemed worth it."

As she said those words, something in my heart signaled the weightiness of this moment. I felt God call to mind passages about "waiting on the Lord," with their promises of his deliverance. I decided that God was telling me, "Don't resign, don't defend yourself, and don't fight back. Just wait." So I did.

My situation with my new boss didn't improve. In fact, for a time it got worse. But my sense of God's word in my life and the truth of God's Word in Scripture gave me strength to endure many tough months. Eventually, about twelve months later, the situation changed dramatically: I was invited to buy the company! Without my having to lift a finger or ever even dreaming of it.

We miss God's voice not, I am sure, because of any lack of desire to hear it but because of a lack of attention. We think the circumstances around us are merely natural occurrences, and so we miss the ways God means to speak to us through them. Our attention is drawn elsewhere, and we become deaf to his voice.

But as we invite God to speak to our hearts in the routine, we learn to identify God's encouragements and gospel revelations, and we begin to distinguish temptations from teachings.

Once we recognize that God's voice is usually a whisper, and once we give up controlling the conversation, we will discover to our delight that "God speaks time and time again" (Job 33:14 ISV), and we can finally distinguish his voice from all the other voices in the world. But his voice will usually seem ordinary, and we'll find that he mostly speaks in everyday events. As someone once said, "The shepherds got to hear glorious angels. All I got were these stinking shepherds!"

The more we *learn* to hear God, the more we will actually hear him—through one of his many methods—as we increasingly recognize his voice in life's commonplace and mundane moments. James Dobson once described his prayer for God's voice in a radio broadcast:

> I get down on my knees and say, "Lord, I need to know what you want me to do, and I am listening. Please speak to me through my friends, books, magazines I pick up and read, and through circumstances."[3]

Nothing Is Too Small for God

I recently heard a depressing dialogue on a Christian radio show. The host had just interviewed the author of a new commentary on Romans. At the end of the interview, the guest mentioned that he was exhausted from the publishing process; he needed an extended vacation but wasn't sure where to go. The host asked, "Have you asked God for direction?" The author responded, "No. I wouldn't want to waste God's time on something as trivial as my vacation."

I can't imagine knowing the book of Romans well enough to write a commentary on it and yet at the same time having so low an opinion of God that I don't want to "bother" him for help with my vacation. In 1961, the author J. B. Phillips wrote a book called *Your God Is Too Small*. It should be required reading for every writer of commentaries, maybe for every seminary student, and certainly for any preacher. If they don't read the book, they should at least meditate on the title.

God is infinite. He is so big that nothing can be too small for him or too trivial. We can ask God to speak to us about anything. That's not to say God will normally tell us which cereal to have for breakfast. But you never know—one morning he might. He's not limited. So why fetter him with our small minds? Let's not lose our expectation to hear God's voice.

After winning his showdown with the priests of Baal (1 Kings 18), Elijah found himself running for his life from the vengeful Queen Jezebel. Victory had turned into despair. Weary and depressed, the prophet lay down beneath a tree, praying that he might die, and then drifted off to sleep. He was shaken from his slumber by a gentle hand. Beside him knelt an angel, offering him a cake of bread and a jar of water. After eating and drinking, Elijah went back to sleep. In a while, again came the angelic touch, and more food and water (1 Kings 19:4–8).

Notice God's attention to the most trivial detail. The angel provided something besides the basic necessities of food and water: he *touched* Elijah. Sometimes, when we are in despair, what we most need is just the basics plus one important thing: maybe sleep, food, and water—and a kind touch. Our God—who is *not* too small—always knows. Always.

This is the God who speaks to us constantly in the world around us. He does not leave us as orphans. He speaks in the wind and waves and kind touches, and through friends and circumstances and even strangers. He talks to us about coworkers, and spouses, and even, sometimes, where to go on vacation.

James tells us that we do not have because we do not ask (or because our motives are wrong). That's a pity, because God delights in speaking to us. Let's not neglect our loyal expectation of him, that he will speak to us through the everyday stuff of our lives. Let's not neglect to ask God for his voice.

Hearing God in the multiple moments of our lives may seem extraordinary to many. But that kind of extraordinary should become our new ordinary—the places we now walk and talk with God.

Chapter 17

God Shouts in His Silence

The tears of God are the meaning of history.
—Nicholas Wolterstorff

Of all the ways God speaks, the one I like least (and fear most) is his silence. The absence of his voice seems to come at the moments I most desperately long for a word. In those moments, his silence feels like God at his cruelest. We tell God that the muteness of his voice is devastating:

> "To you, O Lord, I call; my rock, be not deaf to me, lest, if you be silent to me, I become like those who go down to the pit." (Ps. 28:1)

We cry out to God, we promise to do exactly as he says, and we get nothing. It hardly seems fair.

Paradoxically, God often speaks the loudest in his silence. But his words do not always come as a voice. Later in life, when we remember the silent voice of God, it is those words we come to treasure most. His Spirit breathes life into our experiences, and his silent words somehow take shape in our hearts.

Nothing I've shared with you so far about hearing God through meditation, questions, conversations, brainstorming, and the still, small voice is a foolproof technique. It's not a gimmick. We can't force God's hand, and we certainly can't force him to speak to us. He doesn't respond to our incantations like a dog to its master's command.

He is God, and he speaks and acts in the moments he determines with the methods he knows we most need.

God Works in His Silence

In the mid-nineties, my marriage suffered a vicious attack and almost died. Something happened that drove a wedge between my wife and me. I felt a part of my heart ripping, a splitting of deep inner tissue by a mugger's serrated blade savagely sawing and slashing, blood and guts oozing out of a ruptured chest.

(I put it so graphically to help you understand my desperation. My wife had it worse, because it wasn't events that attacked her. I was her mugger in the dark.)

I prayed to God with a fierce intensity unlike any time before. Despair gripped me with a furious longing for God's voice: his word, guidance, comfort, presence, *anything*. I was in anguish, alone and adrift, a breathing iceberg in the dead cold dark of winter. I wanted God's word with a stark desperation unknown to me. And all I got was silence.

I searched Scripture for answers, I prayed the psalms of desolation, and I asked God for direction. All I got was a monotonous series of "words" delivered to me by friends, pastors, and family. I think these people were well-intentioned, but their words were ill-timed or insensitively given, or I was unable (or unwilling—yes, let's admit that) to hear. They mercilessly interrogated me with the Evangelical Checklist:

- Have you confessed all known sin?
- Have you prayed in faith?
- Have you pleaded the blood of Christ?
- Have you thanked God for his many blessings?
- Have you claimed all God's promises?
- Have you rebuked the Devil?

Those are good questions, great even, and I don't mean to mock them. But none of them touched me. They didn't have a sense of God about them. I tried them nevertheless. I was desperate, emotionally drained, and clinging to any thread of hope. In the end, though, my closest friends and family, mentors and advisors, the words and interrogations, were miserable counselors. I didn't hear from God in any of them. Surrounded by a screaming, shouting, screeching, mocking silence, I despaired.

Then one day a business associate approached me. As far as I could tell, his Christianity was a blend of superstition, New Age, and feeble unorthodox beliefs. But he knew my own beliefs and he sensed my pain. Quietly, gently even, he asked me to tell him what had happened.

As I shared with him the events, misunderstandings, miserable counselors, and my multiple mistakes, he began to cry. Nothing overt, no sniffling or blubbering. He just quietly wept. And I think the incongruity of it is what startled me—tears without moans, crying without shaking, a gentle weeping. The man focused on me as if I were all that mattered, and the tears trickled down his motionless cheeks to his chin and dripped onto his desk.

If ever I met an angel of God disguised as a human, it was on that late afternoon. His silence seemed holy. I can't remember him uttering a single sound. He didn't console, rebuke, question, or suggest a plan. I don't remember even a sympathetic sigh. Just silence and tears.

Nicholas Wolterstorff said, "The tears of God are the meaning of history."[1] In that tearful moment I saw the face of God. The silence made the tears roar. I sensed God's special love for me. Nothing else seemed to matter. I heard zero direction, but I received the comfort of tearful presence.

The recovery of my marriage began that day. I still had much to do. The trail stretched far ahead, and I continued to make a boatload of mistakes. But somehow I knew the trial was over. God did something in my heart. He shifted something through his silence.

Some things need to be shown, not told. Some lessons need the laboratory, not the lecture hall. That day I heard the love of God not through thunderous booms nor through whispered words, but through silent tears.

God's Silence Is Powerful

God's greatest words often come through his seeming silence. God silently sustains the entire universe "by the word of his power" (Heb. 1:3). His word is not always a burning in the heart; often it is inaudible. Sometimes God must use his word as a power that we "hear" only later. Often he has to move a mountain in our hearts, but he can't tell us. He must show us.

Most of the miracles in Scripture resolve external troubles, such as blindness, leprosy, thirst in the desert, and escape from enemies. I can't remember a single instantaneous, miraculous healing of an ill-formed heart. Jesus snaps his fingers and the lame walk, but healing our bitterness takes a process, a series of events in which God's silence shouts to us in our pain.

We hear God's silence in many Scripture stories. Hundreds of years pass between the last verse of Genesis and the first verse of Exodus—and we don't have a single word written about those centuries. The same is true between the end of the Old Testament and the beginning of the New. Yet scholars will tell you that these periods display miraculous works of God. He's still busy. But he's silent.

My two favorite examples of God's silence are in the book of Esther and in the story of Joseph. God is never mentioned in all the book of Esther, not even once. The writer seems to have taken pains to avoid any mention of God. Where Scripture normally couples fasting with prayer, the book of Esther merely says that Jewish exiles fasted.

God is silent in Esther more than in any other biblical account. Yet the thinly veiled message of the entire book is to show God's silent power, his careful orchestration of every person and event so that all the Jews in the entire empire were saved. In God's silence.

The story of Joseph is similar. Before the story of Joseph, all the heroes of the faith get words from God. Adam and Eve walk with God; even the murderer Cain gets to converse with God; and Enoch, Noah, Abraham, and Jacob all hear from God. As for Joseph, he has some dreams (which he never attributes to God), and then the rest of his life is filled with silence.

But the most dramatic spiritual silence in Joseph's life takes place in the little town of Dothan.

Scripture only mentions Dothan twice: once in Elisha's story and once in Joseph's. The two stories describe two different events, and what's odd is, they seem completely contradictory. It's as if Joseph and Elisha are dealing with two different gods on two different planets. Yet both stories reveal God's word of power: one in the display of God's visible power and one in his shouting silence.

In 2 Kings 6, the king of Syria makes repeated plans to raid Israel.

God tells Elisha of the plans, Elisha tells the king of Israel, and the targeted towns are warned and saved. The king of Syria is certain there is a traitor in his camp until one of his counselors tells him the problem lies with Elisha, who "tells the king of Israel the words that you speak in your bedroom."

The Syrian king decides to kill Elisha. He sends crack troops to surround the town of Dothan under the cover of night. In the morning, Elisha's servant awakens and sees the city besieged by a huge army. He rushes to Elisha, who then prays that his servant's eyes would be opened. Suddenly the servant sees that the besieging army is itself surrounded by the horses and chariots of a host of fiery angels. It's a powerful, miraculous work of God.

Isn't that exactly what we want for ourselves—a powerful word or a vision of heavenly hosts? That's the kind of answer we seek. But God has a wider range of responses. Because sometimes we need something *more* than a miraculous intervention that saves us from our enemies.

We see this demonstrated at Dothan, not in Elisha's story but in Joseph's. If Elisha's tale is of the Lord of awesome power, Joseph's almost seems to be the story of Casper the friendly but impotent ghost.

It feels like many of our own stories.

For Joseph, Dothan is a place not of great deliverance but of devastating treachery. When Joseph's older brothers betray him, no angels are on hand to rescue him, no fiery chariots to vanquish his foes. Just vicious brothers who surround Joseph, strip him like you'd skin a beast, beat him nearly to death, and then throw his body into a pit the way a corpse is cast into a grave.

Joseph screams and pleads and begs. And he gets just what you and I fear most. Silence.

Why does God act so powerfully with Elisha while, to all appearances, failing to act at all with Joseph? Is God schizoid or arbitrary? The answer lies in the differing *needs* of Elisha and Joseph. Elisha needed a visible miracle to save him from an external enemy. Joseph needed a heart transplant.

Sometimes all we need is the still, small voice of God. But there are other times when God can't simply tell us an answer. He has to act in a way that we can't understand in the moment. He speaks through our circumstances; then later, as Oswald Chambers puts it, "suddenly, the words become spirit and life because Jesus re-speaks them to us when our circumstances make the words new."[2] God's Spirit breathes new life into the experiences of our lives.

Joseph needed a heart change. More than external rescue, he needed an internal shift that would forever change who he was. God couldn't just tell him. He had to show him.

You see, Joseph's father, Jacob, had ruined the family. He had idolized one wife, Rachel, while marginalizing his other wife, Leah. When Rachel died, Jacob transferred all his loves, dreams, and joys onto Rachel's son Joseph. Jacob treated Leah's sons harshly, or at best ignored them, while idolizing Joseph.

The result was familial cancer: murderously angry brothers and one spoiled brat, Joseph. God had to bring healing to an entire family, the family that would become the patriarchs of Israel. So bit by bit, event by event, God put Joseph through the rock tumbler of trial until Joseph was a gem. But not just Joseph. God also changed the hearts of the brothers.

The ringleader of Joseph's original betrayal had been Judah. He was jealous of his father's affections for his half-brother Joseph. But in a climactic scene at the end of Genesis 44, Judah offers to sacrifice himself for the sake of his other half-brother, Benjamin. Judah has been transformed from a murderous sibling into a self-sacrificing brother.

All because God was silent—seemingly—at the little town of Dothan.

Why Didn't God Act More Dramatically?

Why didn't God send an angel and save everyone, especially Joseph, from the years of hardship? An angel could have shown up in light and glory and shouted, "Everyone, STOP! Jacob, you are ruining your family with favoritism. Joseph, you are turning into an insensitive, narcissistic chump. Brothers, your jealousy has put you on the precipice of slave trade and fratricide. And everyone, a famine fast approaches, so make friends with Pharaoh while you can."

Why didn't God just do *that*?

Because it wouldn't have worked. You and I both know it. We've been told of our "foibles" dozens of times, and we've ignored those messages. Many of those messages may very well have been heavenly messages spoken through your spouse, friends, family, and coworkers. You and I have ignored the words of God. Come on, admit it. We have. And we do.

Oswald Chambers said, "Jesus doesn't take us aside and explain things to us all the time; He explains things to us as we are able to understand them. . . . We can only be used by God after we allow Him to show us the deep, hidden areas of our own character. It is astounding how ignorant we are about ourselves!"[3]

God's silence is often God's voice at its loudest; we just don't hear it. We see it instead. Our anger, little by little, is softened; our narcissism, bit by bit, turns to self-sacrifice; and our greed, dollar by dollar, is transformed into generosity.

> God's silence is often God's voice at its loudest; we just don't hear it. We see it instead.

Maybe God could have saved the family from famine like Elisha was saved by fiery chariots. But only the voice of God in his silence could turn their rocky hearts into gardens.

In the beginning of this chapter, when I said that the times of divine silence become, later in life, the times we treasure most, I meant it. During my incredible hardship in my marriage, I came to know God's love in a way that can never be taken from me. As much as his spoken words, his silent word of power has changed my life.

The seeds of this book were planted when my parents taught me to distinguish God's voice from the cacophony of sounds that surround me. But those seeds were nurtured in the sun and soil and rain of God's silence. It was then, in those harsh times of silence, that I decided to write this book on hearing God.

We are not rocks or trees or suns or stars, insentient and inanimate. We are beings whom God created with souls, apart from God and yet in God, and God in us. He is our very life. Just as in the desert we most cherish water, it is in silence that we most treasure God's voice.

C. S. Lewis wrote, "Can it be that the more perfect the creature is, the further this separation must at some point be pushed? It is saints, not common people, who experience the 'dark night.' It is men and angels, not beasts, who rebel. Inanimate matter sleeps in the bosom of the Father. The 'hiddenness' of God perhaps presses most painfully on those who are in another way nearest to Him."[4]

What Do We Do in the Midst of Silence?

When we seek God's word and all we sense is his absence, how do we rediscover his voice? Remember, there are no gimmicks. But there is wisdom. You may scorn me for speaking out of both sides of my mouth, but I think the Evangelical Checklist is a fine beginning. (I feel right at home among Job's miserable counselors.) Try these:

- Have you confessed all known sin?
- Have you prayed in faith?
- Have you pleaded the blood of Christ?
- Have you thanked God for his many blessings?
- Have you claimed all God's promises?
- Have you rebuked the Devil?

Repentance

Sin really is an obstacle to hearing God, especially when we willfully reject his word. We earnestly pray for God's guidance, he tells us to repent to our wife for our arrogance, and in our arrogance we ignore his instruction. Then we ask God to speak again. But God is giving us our manna one day at a time, and today's manna is repentance. Don't worry about tomorrow's words until you've polished off what's presently on your plate.

Faith

Scriptural faith is not the "Name It, Claim It" positive thinking of modern televangelists. Faith is an inner assurance of God's love, care, and orchestration of our lives. We can pray *for* faith and we can pray *in* faith that God speaks in whispers and sometimes in our pains. Ask God for a heart that trusts in him above all things.

It's a prayer he loves to grant.

The Blood of Christ

When I hear silence—that is, when I sense God's absence—I try to remember the cross. Not salvation only, but the *meaning* of the cross: that sin is man substituting himself for God, and salvation is God substituting himself for man.[5] On the cross, Jesus got the silence we deserve so that we get the voice that Jesus deserved; Jesus took our place so we can hear the voice of the Father as his sons. When I plead the blood of Christ, I remind myself that he always does more than I ask or think.

Gratitude

God has spoken to me when I list his blessings to me: my wife and kids, the times I've heard him in the past, his undeserved love, the sun and snow, my pets, and my love for writing. When I feel his silence, I take out and reread Ann Voskamp's book *One Thousand Gifts*. It has never failed to speak to me.

Gratitude doesn't always give me the words I want, but it always comforts me.

Claiming Promises

The purpose of claiming promises is to run our eyes up from the beams of sunlight (the blessings) to the Sun, to see the Illuminator more than just the illumination. Promises are only as good as the one who makes them. That's why we meditate on Scripture: it's to come to know the nature and person of God. When I'm bereft of words, I pray Psalm 23: "The Lord is my shepherd; I shall not want . . ."

As I reflect on the character of a shepherd, God reminds me that his nature—who he is—will never allow him to abandon me. Even in silence.

Spiritual Warfare

In Daniel 10, Daniel seeks God's voice. An angel appears and says that God heard Daniel the minute he prayed and sent the angel as a messenger, but "the prince of the kingdom of Persia withstood me twenty-one days" (Dan. 10:13). There are evil forces that oppose God's word. Of course there are! But God has given us authority, and we can tell our enemy, "Be gone, in the name of Christ." It's good to have a friend or two assist you; not because you lack the authority (which is given to all believers) but because the faith of our friends often strengthens the weakness of our own faith.

But don't work yourself into a lather. It isn't up to us. It is Christ's work, not our own. He is faithful, and he will do it.

When my checklist sputters, I reread the story of Esther or Joseph. I am wonderfully comforted to see God's unfailing action in the absolute stillness of a voice in both stories. It strengthens my hope to consider that God is working more powerfully than I can imagine. I remember that neither Joseph nor Esther had the slightest clue how their lives would conclude.

And I ask God what he might be saying in his silence.

The Lord Is Our Shepherd

Elisabeth Elliot tells the story of seeing a modern-day shepherd treat his sheep with antiseptics to save them from disease. She wrote,

> One by one John seized the rams by their curled horns and flung them into the antiseptic [a putrid, black liquid]. They would struggle to climb out the side and Mack [the Scottish Collie] would snarl and snap at their faces to force them back in. Just as they were about to climb up the ramp at the far end, John caught them by the horns with a wooden implement, spun them around, forced them under again, and held them—ears, eyes and nose submerged for a few seconds.
>
> I've had some experiences in my life which have made me feel very sympathetic to those poor rams—I couldn't figure out any reason for the treatment that I was getting from the Shepherd that I trusted. And he didn't give me a hint of explanation.
>
> As I watched the struggling sheep I thought, If only there was some way to explain to these poor animals what was being done to them! But such knowledge is too wonderful for them— it is high, they cannot attain unto it. So far as they could see, there was no point whatsoever.[6]

Yet there is a point. God is beyond us, and sometimes he simply has to act, to show us before he can explain. After all, none of the disciples understood Christ's cross, did they? Would we really want a God who waits for our understanding before taking action? We'd still be slaves in Egypt.

God does not play games with us. If we need to hear him, he will speak. Always. His silence usually means he is acting in ways we cannot now understand. Just as in the lives of Joseph and Esther, his silence is a prelude to wonders we cannot now imagine.

Chapter 18

The God Who Guides

And he went out, not knowing whither he went.
—Hebrews 11:8 (KJV)

Living a life of faith means never knowing where you are being led. But it [also means] loving and knowing the One who is leading. It is literally a life of faith, not of understanding and reason—a life of knowing Him who calls us to go. Faith is rooted in the knowledge of a Person.
—Oswald Chambers

We're finally going to talk about how to hear God's voice for guidance. And let's be honest, this is the reason we read books on hearing God. We seek to hear his voice with one purpose in mind: to get his direction. I hope by now we recognize that our *real* need—beyond any *perceived* needs—is a conversational relationship with God, to walk and talk with him. If that is all we have, it would be enough.

But it *isn't* all we have. Part of the heart of God is his desire to guide us in our walk through life with him. But recognizing his guidance requires maturity on our part, a growing ability to distinguish his quiet whispers from the shouting clamor of other voices. A daily conversation with God teaches us the sound, tone, and quality of his voice; it equips us to identify his spoken directions.

But God rarely limits his guiding voice to a single method. Rather, like a master painter, he uses an artful mix of brushstrokes and palette, sometimes speaking, other times orchestrating, oftentimes through counsel, and frequently even in his silence. God's primary purpose is to deepen his

> God rarely limits his guiding voice to a single method.

relationship with us. He doesn't give us a paint-by-number scheme for guidance. Each of our lives is his masterpiece, and each masterpiece is painted with different colors and varying brushstrokes. Let's not limit God's guidance to dime-store paint kits.

Because God's directional words are so artfully diverse, I've decided to adopt a different approach with this chapter. Rather than outlining principles and rules, this whole chapter is a story, the story of God's directional portraiture of my life. I will walk you through God's guidance journey with me. As you see God's painting of my life, I hope you will recognize his brushstrokes in yours as well.

There May Not Be an Immediate Answer

Early in 2006, I thought I heard God call me to leave the company that had employed me for the previous twenty-five years. A small group of friends helped me discern that sense. After eleven months of prayer and discussion, I tendered my resignation to my business partners. The bulk of the following year, 2007, was spent finding and training my replacement.

On January 1, 2008, I woke up to a new morning that included no clients, no phone calls, no meetings, no employees, no urgent tasks, no job, and no paychecks. And absolutely no idea what I was supposed to do with the rest of my life.

You see, that small gang of discerning friends spent those eleven months asking the question, what should Sam do after he leaves his company? Our question went answerless.

We had no shortage of ideas. We discussed graduate school, ordination, college ministry, men's ministry, and inner-city outreach. We argued, laughed, prayed, cajoled, persuaded, and shared strong opinions. Every idea was explored. But no answer appeared.

Finally, in the eleventh month, my friend Phil proposed that we split our discussion into two questions: Should Sam leave now? and, What should Sam do in the future? When Phil asked, "Should Sam leave now?" we had instant, unanimous accord: each one of us agreed that God was calling me to leave. When Phil asked, "What should Sam do in the future?" we again had instant, unanimous accord: each one of us agreed that we were totally clueless.

That's why I awoke that January morning to an empty to-do list. After two years of seeking God's guidance, I was still clueless. God had called me *away* from something, but I had no idea what God was calling me *to*.

There May Not Be an Obvious Answer

This was not my first experience with cluelessness (just ask my family). In 1982, after serving overseas in missions, to the best of my discernment I heard God say, "Not now," to missions. So I returned to the States. Until that moment, I had always imagined a life of mission work; no other idea had ever been considered.

My university studies did little to prepare me for a career. A degree in sixteenth- and seventeenth-century European intellectual history attracted few employers, and studies of philosophy and Hebrew found even fewer openings. My bank account had enough cash for about six weeks, so I found odd jobs to keep me afloat as I looked for a professional occupation.

As I began my career search, I read this famous proverb: "Trust in the Lord, not your own ideas; acknowledge him in all your plans, and he will direct your paths" (Prov. 3:5-6 swp). Meditating on this proverb produced my paraphrase above and the following simple steps for getting God's guidance:

After prayer, counsel, and wisdom: *make a plan.*
Then: *commit that plan to God.*
Finally: *let God direct your path.*

But committing our plan to God means recognizing that he will frequently guide us down paths our original maps never envisioned. We trust in God and his goodness to direct us, not in our own ideas for our lives; we especially don't trust our own plans. Plans are just nice starting points to get us moving.

God's most common guidance is done naturally, through nonobvious means. The hiddenness of his guidance means we will take risks, learn through trial and error, and continue to be alert to God's gentle nudges. This is perfectly fine. It means we remain in conversational contact with God.

After leaving missions, I put my three-step breakdown of the proverb into motion. I talked with a career counselor, enrolled in a job-search program, took personality and aptitude tests, networked with scores of contacts, and read books on résumé writing and managing the interview. I even read *Dress for Success*. (Don't laugh. It helped me more than my history degree.) In other words, I exercised wisdom in order to create a plan to commit to God.

I found God's guidance through wise reasoning, advice from friends and counselors, examination of my skills and personality, extended prayer, and trial and error.

My very first professional job originally appeared to be an excellent fit. But after starting it, I hated it. Eight months later, I was hired by a rapidly growing video company that needed internal organization. This was a job I loved, and in it I learned to program computers for a variety of business operations. Unfortunately, the company moved to Hollywood after only a year, and I wanted to stay in Michigan.

A local software company soon hired me because of the computer skills I had gained while organizing the video company. I remained with that software company for the next two and a half decades. It was a terrific fit for my skill set. I arrived there by God's word (telling me to leave missions), counsel, reasonably wise plans that I committed to God, and risk and trial and error.

God directed my path to an industry, software, that I had never imagined and that my plans failed to envision.

We May Need to "Try On the Dress"

I'm a boring clothes shopper. When I need to replace my blue jeans or black shirt, my trip to the store is swift. I make a beeline for the right aisles, snatch the articles, and sprint for the cashier. If the Olympics offered medals for shopping, I'd win a gold for the fifty-yard dash, not the marathon.

I once took my daughter shopping for her senior homecoming dress. She took half a dozen or so into the changing room. She'd come out wearing one, and then model it for me and the mirror. Dresses that looked good on the rack sometimes clashed with her coloring or just didn't fit. Other dresses that seemed ordinary on the rack looked beautiful on my daughter. (Of course, *everything* looks great on my daughter, but some dresses looked better than others.)

The "commit your plan to God" wisdom works well when you finally have a plan to commit, but what do you do when you can't choose a plan? How do we find a winning strategy between competing alternatives when all the choices seem equally attractive? We use the same wisdom: we make a plan . . . to make a plan, commit it to God, and trust him to direct.

The secret to making good plans (that we can commit to God) is to see ourselves in the dress. We make a plan (try on a dress). We commit it to God (model it in the mirror). And then we let God direct our path— even when we discover that the dress that looked great on the rack looks awful in the mirror.

How do we try on a plan? When I chose my first professional job, I had two competing offers. One involved writing user manuals and the other entailed consulting with companies during their high-tech purchase decisions. Both jobs offered similar salaries and both exercised a subset of my skills. So how did I decide?

I imagined for a day that I had chosen option number one. I put on the dress and looked in the mirror. I asked God to help me see my life in that choice: What would my daily activities include? With whom would I interact? How would I get along with the colleagues I had met in the interview process? Which elements of the job resonated with me, and which ones seemed discordant? In other words, did the job fit me, was it comfortable, how did I look in it, and was it "me"?

Then the next day I tried on the other dress.

Both times, I brainstormed with God by asking him to open my eyes as I looked in the mirror. But what I've described is a different sort of brainstorming. Instead of simultaneously juggling all the pros and cons of each choice, we pick an option and then live in it for a day as though the decision has been made (some decisions may require living "in the dress" for longer than a day). It's like a debriefing in advance. We prayerfully imagine and then examine an after-action report.

Then we compare notes. One of the jobs provided me with little customer involvement; I'd spend most of my time in a cubicle. The other meant time in customers' offices, asking questions about their needs, budgets, and technology competence. The first company had great management while the second seemed to run in disarray. Yet despite its management concerns, I realized that the second company's daily activity of talking with customers suited me far better than the isolation of writing user manuals. That was the plan I chose to commit to God.

I arrived at it by trying on some dresses—or in my case, their manly counterpart: I ran my fifty-yard dash in a kilt.

God Orchestrates Our Lives

In January of 2008, I was again experiencing directional cluelessness. This time, however, I felt more lost than ever. I had heard God tell me to leave my company (*check*), and I had enlisted wise counsel (*check*), but every idea for a plan left a check in my spirit. No idea resonated as a starting plan to commit to God; every dress looked awful.

I was desperate. I had left a successful career in order to . . . well, I didn't know what. When people asked me what I did for an occupation, I'd respond, "I *used* to be an executive . . ." No present tense. My cluelessness, and my desperation, continued for another fifteen months.

Forty years ago my dad preached a sermon on two of the ways that God guides us: guidance he *speaks* and guidance he *orchestrates*. My dad said that we're always looking for God's voice, but God's primary direction is found in his careful orchestration of our lives. He said that we'll discover God's fingerprints all over our lives if we simply stop to dust for them.

We see this orchestration in the lives of Joseph, David, and Esther, but what about *our* lives? Does God still act the same way today? Does he help us as a real father would? Oswald Chambers writes,

We can all see God in exceptional things [and people], but it requires the growth of spiritual discipline to see God in every detail. Never believe that the so-called random events of life are anything less than God's appointed order. Be ready to discover His divine designs anywhere and everywhere.[1]

I had always pictured God's direction of our lives as a kind of *event coordination*. I imagined God managing Joseph's life through a variety of positions leading up to his final rank as prime minister of Egypt. External event coordination, however, is child's play for God.

God is also our *skills trainer*. He personally arranges experiences that train us for future positions he has designed for us. God trains the young boy David to

- fight Goliath using unconventional means;
- learn court etiquette while performing as a musician; and
- develop great friendships (because of King Saul's persecution).

God was David's personal curriculum advisor. He arranged laboratory experiences to foster the skills David needed.

God also, most importantly, quietly orchestrates character, or *heart development*. Besides events and then skills training, he also arranges experiences to develop the spiritual maturity we need to handle success. Esther's rise to royalty was the result of Queen Vashti's defiance coupled with Esther's sweet nature. God's guidance transformed Esther's heart to the point that she, like Vashti, risked her life in a public act of valor.

Event coordination, skills training, and heart development: our Father attends to all three of them in our lives. He carefully orchestrates our times, seasons, and experiences. He nurtures our abilities. And he strengthens our character.

What Guidance Have We Seen So Far?

Think about the different ways, both verbal and nonverbal, that you have seen God's guidance in different moments of your life. Let's recap some of his methods:

He speaks *directly*—such as the times when he asked me to leave the mission field and my company.

He speaks through the *counsel of others*—through the smart, unbiased (or at least differently biased) advice of friends and counselors.

He guides through *wisdom*—using practical resources when looking for a career, and committing our plans to God.

He helps us *see ourselves* in the dress in order to make a plan.

He arranges the *events* of our lives to bring us into his plans.

He *trains our abilities*—as in the lives of Moses, Samuel, and David.

He *shapes our hearts*—guiding us the way he did Esther when her strengthened character allowed her to proclaim at great personal risk, "If I perish, I perish."

And of course he guides us through Scripture. While Scripture won't tell us to study software engineering, it will curb our bank-robbing career. Hearing God through the Bible gives us almost daily guidance: repenting to our spouse for neglect, boldly battling cultural creep in our lives, and raising kids.

In your personal journey, what are some of the ways you've experienced God's guidance in the midst of your circumstances? Maybe you weren't even aware of his guidance at the time—that's often the case—but in hindsight, you can clearly see how he has directed your path and spoken to you in unique and creative ways.

Listen to Your Life

After I left my company, I tried every method for getting God's guidance that I knew of. I prayed, got counsel, examined my motivations and abilities (which eliminated fashion modeling), and studied Scripture (which eliminated grand theft auto). And I still didn't know what to do.

When my wife told a friend that I was "retired," it angered me. I didn't leave work to retire at the age of fifty. I had left to start a new career. I just didn't know what it was. My directionless life embarrassed me. *How could I have been so stupid as to leave a job without a plan?*

I prayed, begged, and pleaded with God, *What do you want me to do?* Then one day, in a moment as ordinary as any other, I heard God turn my question back on me. I literally sensed the direct question: "Sam, what do *you* want to do?"

My initial response was disappointment. "No way. You got me into this. I want a spoken direction or some orchestration." Then suspicion: this "what do you want?" seemed suspiciously unspiritual, like a copout from God. I had sacrificed a rewarding career to follow his lead. And he wouldn't lead.

Besides, what kind of word from God is "Do what you want"? I had spent much of my life trying, and failing, to crush my desires. All my biggest blunders in life had been the times when I *listened* to my desires, with minor to catastrophic consequences.

But that sense from God—*My direction can be found in your desires*—persisted and intensified.

I *really* wanted discernment on this word, so I asked my friends for more counsel. Over time it became not only clear but obvious: Of course God directs through our desires—our purified desires, that is, not the desires of the flesh. Don't we do the same with our kids? Would we ask our literary-minded child to become a rocket scientist, or our mathematically inclined child to be a greeting-card salesperson? And wouldn't our heavenly Father be even better at this than we are?

"No one ever disbelieved God because he promised too little."[2] We all disbelieve God because he promises too much.

Frederick Buechner urges us to examine our lives to understand God's guidance. He wrote, "There is no event so commonplace but that God is present within it, always hiddenly, always leaving you room to recognize him or not to recognize him, but all the more fascinatingly because of that. . . . Listen to your life."[3]

Walk with God in Conversation

I began college with the intention of studying nuclear physics. One history class—taken to fulfill requirements but I think orchestrated by God—changed my life. My study of intellectual history prepared me to examine more deeply the hidden, inarticulate beliefs that drive how people think and behave. And I loved it.

I fell into the software industry through a mixture of God's voice and orchestration. In twenty-five years as an analyst, I learned to dig beneath the surface of a client's request to discover what they really wanted but couldn't articulate. And I learned to express complicated computer concepts to nontechnical people.

I've learned that I love to reflect deeply on the beliefs that drive our culture, and I love to express what I hear God say in Scripture, meditation, and conversation. I absolutely love it. I can think of not one thing in this world that I would rather do. Except now I do it through exploring our deepest heart beliefs instead of seventeenth-century history or twenty-first-century software applications.

God's guidance comes to our lives through an artful mix of speaking and counsel; of his shaping our hearts, forming our abilities, and orchestrating our desires; and of his written Word. God wants a relationship with us, so he gives us no magic guidance formula. Sometimes he speaks clearly: "Sam, leave your company." At other times he speaks through wisdom gained from counsel and study. And still other times he seems silent. In all of it, all the while, he is guiding, directing, and shaping us.

I wanted to be a missionary, but I spent the vast majority of my adult life as a software executive, and then I became a writer. But I'm not *just* a writer. Someone once observed, "Writing is detangling your thoughts through your fingers." God has created in me a longing—a gripping desire—for thought-detanglement; to observe, study, and ponder the deepest issues we face. And then to express what I see.

One of the greatest needs I see is for believers to hear God in an everyday relationship. This book is my detanglement of all that my parents taught me and all that God has woven into me.

Along the way I have seen thunderstorms and stillness, darkness and daylight. God's companionship has been with me throughout. I never imagined or planned my life as it has turned out: missionary to software executive to thought-detangler. In the end, all I needed was a conversational relationship with God, a daily walk with the Creator in the cool of the garden.

God invites us all, "Walk with me."

Do you know God's call on your life?
Do you sense his purpose for you?
Do you know what you are doing here?
Do you hear his voice in conversation?
Do you see his daily orchestration?

Answers to all of these questions, and many more, are found in walking with God. A conversational relationship is God's heart for us. God didn't save us just so we can be good. He redeemed us to be with him, to talk and chat and converse with our Father. God longs to speak to us even more than we want to hear him. Look at what it cost him to accomplish it. It's always been that way, ever since God called to Adam in hiding, "Where are you?"

God calls to each of us, "Walk with me." Let's respond to his invitation for intimacy, connection, and conversation.

Appendix A

Answers to the Arguments

Anyone who rejects the general counsels of Scripture is in fact planning not to be guided by God and cannot rely on being able to be delivered from his or her difficulties by obtaining God's input on particular occasions.
—Dallas Willard

Let us test and examine our ways, and return to the Lord!
—Lamentations 3:40

Several streams of theology within the church today reject any notion of God speaking outside of his written Word. I personally identify with many beliefs within those streams—though they may not wish to identify with me!—but they are mistaken in this area.

If you ask Christians whether it is possible to hear God today, you will usually hear a version of one of these three answers: (a) "Yes, God certainly speaks today"; (b) "I think so, but I'm not sure because I've heard good arguments against it, and it's never happened to me"; and (c) "God only speaks through his written Word."

I've written this book for Christians who believe you can hear God's voice and want to hear him more, and for believers who want to hear him but don't and who are slightly swayed by opposing arguments. This is a book designed to help Christians deepen their relationship with God. It's not primarily designed to be a defense.

I doubt that the third category of Christians—those who reject any divine communication outside of Scripture—will find my arguments persuasive. That's okay; fair is fair. I haven't found their arguments convincing either. This appendix is not an attempted *tour de force* apologetic. It simply reminds believers that there are excellent arguments *against* the arguments that say God no longer speaks today.

In the point/counterpoint discussions that follow, each section summarizes one argument against God speaking today and then follows with answers to the argument.

Upon the completion of the Bible, God no longer speaks *directly* outside of Scripture.

This position holds that in this "post-miraculous, Christian age," God no longer speaks outside his written Word. It argues that Scripture itself claims that God will no longer give us extrabiblical words. An example of passages used to support this position comes from the beginning of the book of Hebrews:

> Long ago, at many times and in many ways, God spoke to our fathers by the prophets, but in these last days he has spoken to us by his Son, whom he appointed the heir of all things, through whom also he created the world. He is the radiance of the glory of God and the exact imprint of his nature, and he upholds the universe by the word of his power. After making purification for sins, he sat down at the right hand of the Majesty on high, having become as much superior to angels as the name he has inherited is more excellent than theirs (Heb. 1:1–4).

Some believers contend this passage teaches that (a) it was only long ago that God spoke in many ways; (b) those "many times and ways" are now overshadowed by the infinitely superior words spoken by God's Son, Jesus, and by the rest of the New Testament; and (c) when Jesus "sat down," it symbolized the *completeness* of his redemption, miraculous works, and personal speaking.

What are we to say?

Yes, Hebrews does teach that Jesus is superior in all ways, and that his teaching is the final word of salvation. In fact, the writer later explains that the old covenant, with its temple, sacrifices, and priests, was a mere shadow of the reality of the redemption Jesus brought, and that many of the "many times and many ways" pointed directly to Jesus (Heb. 8:5).

When Jesus "sat down," his redemption was complete. Past prophets (Moses, Isaiah, Jeremiah, etc.) spoke of a future salvation, and their words met their *fulfillment* in Jesus Christ alone. There cannot be further words of redemption: "Salvation belongs to our God who sits on the throne, and to the Lamb!" (Rev. 7:10). The Lamb has been sacrificed and resurrected. It is finished.

But nowhere in the passage does God even hint that he will not speak today. The messengers of old spoke more than words of redemption; they also spoke *personal* words of repentance (the prophet Nathan to David), guidance (God himself telling Abraham to leave Ur), instruction for naming a child (the angel Gabriel to the father of John the Baptist), and comfort (the angel to Elisha).

Why would God stop speaking such words to us today? Will Jesus be *less* personal than he was before his incarnation?

Scripture is all we need to be complete.

Some believers argue that Scripture itself teaches us that the God-breathed words of the Bible are all the words that God promises: in them we are complete, and in them we have all we need for a life of good service. The most common passage used to support this argument is Paul's second letter to Timothy:

> Continue in what you have learned and have firmly believed, knowing from whom you learned it and how from childhood you have been acquainted with the sacred writings, which are able to make you wise for salvation through faith in Christ Jesus. All Scripture is breathed out by God and profitable for teaching, for reproof, for correction, and for training in righteousness, that the man of God may be complete, equipped for every good work. (2 Tim. 3:14–17)

Supporters of this position argue that extrabiblical words cannot be needed since Scripture itself says that the Bible is all we need to be complete. If we are *complete* in Scripture, then we cannot need—and God would not provide—a single word more. Complete means done!

What are we to say?

I completely, wholeheartedly, and unequivocally agree that Scripture is God-breathed Word, and it contains all that we need for truth, reproof, correction, and training in righteousness.

But this means we have to look at *all* of what Scripture teaches, and it teaches many things:

- We need faith for salvation, faith in the saving work of Christ.
- Jesus is the divine, preexistent Son of God.
- We have hope of a new heavens and earth and of our own bodily resurrection.
- There are right and wrong ways to behave toward God and other humans.
- Creation once was perfect, and then it was corrupted by human rebellion.

Scripture also teaches us about the heart of God, a God who loves us to the shocking extent that he calls us his children, his betrothed, and his friends. If we believe in the completeness of Scripture—that God revealed what we need and that *we need all that God revealed*—we must also believe in its self-revealed God who delights in a relationship with his children.

Scripture does not teach a deist god who set the world spinning and then sat back and watched from afar. No. It reveals a Father who walks and talks with us in the cool of the garden—a God who comes to meet with Adam and Eve in the garden. Even after their sin.

God wants a conversational relationship with us.

If we believe 2 Timothy 3:14-17, then we must believe in a God who also desires to talk with us personally. We can't have it both ways; we can't believe in the rules and doctrines and ignore the heart of the Father revealed on every page.

We cannot add to or subtract from Scripture.

Supporters of this position argue that any personal, direct word from God is an addition to his Word and thus contradicts his warnings found in a few of the last verses of Revelation:

> I warn everyone who hears the words of the prophecy of this book: *if anyone adds to them,* God will add to him the plagues described in this book, and *if anyone takes away from the words* of the book of this prophecy, God will take away his share in the tree of life and in the holy city. (Rev. 22:18–19)

What are we to say?

It's true that we are not to add to, or subtract from, God's words. But that passage means we cannot add to his words of salvation or subtract from his words of morality (or truth, doctrine, etc.). Woe to any of us who add moralistic works to earn salvation or who remove sexual norms because our culture laughs at them.

But God's warning in no way limits God from speaking to me, that ten-year-old atheist, outside of a Bible study. Neither does God restrict himself from calling me away from ministry as a twenty-five-year-old and then back into ministry as a fifty-year-old. Those words neither added to nor subtracted from his truth.

Dallas Willard maintains, "Nothing in Scripture, in reason or in the very nature of things asserts *why any or all of these [past biblical characters'] types of experience might not be used by God today.* . . . There is nothing *in* Scripture to indicate that the biblical modes of God's communication with humans have been superseded or abolished by either the presence of the church or the close of the scriptural canon."[1]

God commands that we neither add to nor subtract from the Bible. But his command does not limit God himself from speaking to us in the cool of the evening. It doesn't even pretend to.

Too many people want personal, direct words more than they want Scripture.

This position argues that too many people today abandon the hard work of discerning the rich Word of God in favor of spontaneous, inspirational pick-me-up messages from God. Only in God's Word do we have a true revelation of salvation and the certainty of truth.

What are we to say?

Far too many believers in fact do not go to Scripture for the life in them that God promises. This is not only sad, it is also dangerous. God speaks life into us through his written Word. This is why so many of the chapters in this book are dedicated to helping us hear God as he self-reveals in Scripture. In his Word we have real life. Let's not shortchange all that God means for us to have.

Besides, Jesus lived and died by the words of the Bible. Ten percent of all the words of Jesus shared in the Gospels are direct quotes from the Old Testament Scriptures. If the Bible was such a part of Jesus's own thought life, then they are just what we need as well.

I believe in hearing God today just as I believe in miracles today. But E. Stanley Jones has a warning about miracles that should be applied to personal words as well:

> I believe in miracle, but not too much miracle, for too much miracle would weaken us, make us dependent on miracle instead of our obedience. . . . Just enough miracle to let us know He is there, but not too much, lest we depend on [miracles] when we should depend on our own initiative and on His orderly processes for our development.[2]

God's primary, orderly process for our development is found in hearing him in his written Word.

Personal words from God are not infallible; only Scripture is.

This claim argues that personal words from God are subject to all manner of error, that they don't have the certainty of Scripture, and that basing any decision on these words can easily lead us into theological or moral error. They point to Paul's second letter to Timothy:

> For the time is coming when people will not endure sound teaching, but having itching ears they will accumulate for themselves teachers to suit their own passions, and will turn away from listening to the truth and wander off into myths. (2 Tim. 4:3–4)

Supporters of this argument have an ever-expanding list of case examples extensive enough to rival the Library of Congress, filled with believers who abandoned morality, cult leaders claiming to be messiahs, and theologians spouting heresies.

What are we to say?

Only in Scripture can we be absolutely sure of divine authorship. If we hear any direct word from God, our level of certainty that God has spoken to us is directly proportional to the degree to which that word conforms to Scripture. So we must approach every word we hear with humility and lay it before Scripture.

Our fallibility should make us humble in hearing God, not resistant to hearing him. Most of the heresies seen over the centuries have been developed by highly educated theologians, often those teaching in seminaries. Scripture itself is infallible, but its students aren't.

Does human theological fallibility mean we should stop students from studying theology? By no means! It means we should have our very best spiritual minds doing their very best theological work and then leading the rest of us into a better, more accurate understanding of the Bible. Likewise, instead of teaching that we can't hear God because we aren't infallible, we should have our best spiritual minds teaching us how to hear God and leading the world in discerning his voice.

Why would we abandon *hearing God* to the less mature with the argument that "it might be dangerous"? Driving to work is dangerous, but we don't get rid of our cars; we improve our driving.

And There Are More Arguments for
Hearing God Today

The sections above summarize today's most common arguments against hearing God, followed by answers to those arguments. There are even more arguments in favor of God's speaking to believers today. I find myself, however, in an awkward position. While I strongly disagree with believers who claim that God only speaks through Scripture, I am also strongly sympathetic toward them, because I believe that most believers, including me, barely scratch the surface of the life-enriching Word of God found in the Bible. If I had to choose between hearing God "directly" and hearing God in Scripture, I would pick Scripture, where God's richest, most profound, and life-sustaining words are found.

But God doesn't make us choose.

Below are more reasons for hearing God directly. However, I preface them with this caveat: let's not dwell on conversational words at the expense of his written Word. Both are important, but it's the Scriptures alone that are fully reliable.

That being said, here are additional arguments in favor of hearing God speak directly.

God wants relationship with us.

From Genesis to Revelation, the theme of Scripture is relationship with God. God made us in his image, and that image is of a relational, triune God. Christianity is not a religion of moralism, earning access to God through our good works, and redemption is not merely about cleansing us of sin. That redemption is necessary in order to restore us to a relationship with God. But to see salvation as nothing more than cleansing is like admiring a feast without participating. God has invited us to eat at his banquet, not just observe.

Adam's loneliness in the garden of Eden—Paradise!—was not a sign of a weakness. Adam was lonely in the garden because he was perfect. He was made in the image of God.

When God performed Adam and Eve's wedding ceremony, his sermon was, "Therefore a man shall leave his father and his mother and hold fast to his wife, and they shall become one flesh" (Gen. 2:24). In

Ephesians, Paul says that God's short sermon was really about our relationship with God: "This mystery is profound, and I am saying that it refers to Christ and the church" (Eph. 5:32).

The pages of Scripture overflow with God's revelation of his desire for, and our need of, a relationship with him. The curtain to the temple's Holy of Holies represented the barrier to our relationship with God, and when Jesus died, the curtain was torn asunder. We are restored to God's intended purpose for humanity: a conversational relationship with God, a walk with the Creator in the cool of the day.

God wants friendship with us. To say that God has self-limited his own speaking to his written Word doesn't even sound like the God who revealed himself in that written Word.

We hear God when his Scriptures are explained.

I once heard a pastor preach on the *kenosis*: Jesus's emptying himself for us, described in Philippians 2:5–8. It was a terrific sermon, and God spoke to me through the pastor's explanation. The pastor, however, believes that God restricts himself to speaking only in Scripture. If God is so self-restricting, why did the pastor have to add his own voice to God's words? Why didn't the pastor simply repeat the verses over and over until we "got" it?

It's because God still speaks directly to us through other believers, even when they simply expound on his Word.

It's why I can hear God's voice when I read books such as *The Imitation of Christ, My Utmost for His Highest*, and Augustine's *Confessions*. God speaks to us through his people, people from the past, the present, and sometimes even through strangers.

The Word became flesh.

In the beginning of the gospel of John, God declared that Jesus was his Word made flesh. In doing so, God revealed the personal nature of his Word. It's more than letters and paragraphs *about* God; John 1 declares that a relationship of communication is core to God's nature.

Just as human marriage is a divine explanation of our relationship with Christ, so the Scriptures are a divine revelation of our relationship with God. The incarnate Word declares that our relationship with God is a conversational relationship. Our God is not the cold, impersonal "force" described in *Star Wars*; our God is communication incarnate. Dallas Willard writes,

> The close of the scriptural canon marks the point in the (still ongoing) divine–human conversation where the principles and doctrines that form the substance of Christian faith and practice are so adequately stated in human language that nothing more needs to be said *in general*. Biblical Christians believe that nothing further will be said by God to extend or contradict those principles. But biblical Christians are not just people who hold certain beliefs *about* the Bible. They are also people who *lead the kind of life demonstrated* in the Bible: a life of personal, intelligent interaction with God. Anything less than this makes a mockery of the priesthood of the believer.[3]

God wants our whole person.

The heresy of the Enlightenment was its deification of reason. That heresy infected the church to the point where reason became the sole arbiter of Scripture study. But let's use some reason here: Scripture itself teaches there are spiritual mysteries that can only be understood by God's *direct disclosure*. Paul declares that "the mystery was made known to [him] by revelation" and that it was "revealed" by the Holy Spirit (Eph. 3:3, 5).

Reason was the reason why John Wesley was ostracized by the church leaders of his time. "They argued that authentic faith is ultimately rational—that the beginning and end of faith come in one's understanding, in rational conviction. . . . For [them] all the Christian needed was to be found through the logical teachings of the church."[4]

In contrast, the *postmodern* heresy reacts to reason and now deifies feelings. We just want to *feel* God's presence; we want spontaneous utterances that comfort and emotional euphoria that uplifts.

The good news is that God wants our *whole* being. Christianity is not less than rational and it's not less than experience: it's the whole package. Scripture commands us to love God with all our heart, soul, mind, and strength (Mark 12:30). That's everything. Willard argues,

> Speaking pastorally, I believe one of the greatest harms church leaders can do to those in their care is to convince them that God isn't going to meet them personally or that he is meeting them only if *the leaders* approve of what's happening. If our gospel does not free the individual for a unique life of spiritual adventure in living with God daily, we simply have not entered fully into the good news that Jesus brought.[5]

God always provides more than we can ask or even imagine according to his power that is at work in us (Eph. 3:20). God wants to speak personally with a voice that is personal, rational, experiential, and conversational. And that's just what I ask or imagine he will do based on his written Word.

Imagine what God will do when he does *more* than we ask or imagine.

Questionable and Excessive Practices

For the time is coming when people will not endure sound teaching,
but having itching ears they will accumulate for themselves
teachers to suit their own passions, and will turn away
from listening to the truth and wander off into myths.
—2 Timothy 4:3–4

Some Christians resist the notion of God speaking to us outside of Scripture because of the theological reservations discussed in appendix A. But I suspect even more believers avoid the practice of hearing God because of all the excesses they've witnessed. They see the results of immoderation, and they want no part of it.

The crazy customs some of us practice chase away believers who would otherwise be open to the many and various ways God speaks. Let's listen to their concerns. The more purely we can demonstrate what it means to hear God, the more positive and persuasive an effect we will have on the skeptical. Believers with grave concerns won't listen to us when we are silent about the eccentricities in our midst.

For those who resist the idea of hearing God because you've been turned off by oddball behaviors: we need your balanced perspective. You too practice some elements of hearing God. Otherwise, how can some believe they are "called" to ministry while others feel they aren't? Both read the same passages. Some verses call out to you, "Join full-time ministry," while those same passages say something else to others. Please join us in the discussion. If nothing else, teach us how you recognize God's voice in those passages.

Let's listen to each other. Those who see the dangers, help us hear God in Scripture even more. Those who believe in hearing God directly, let's examine ourselves for intemperate excesses. Together we can lead others in hearing God as he intended. Let's walk together as we walk with God.

Below are common examples of immoderations accompanied by suggestions for how to handle them.

Self-Importance

I know a man who believes God called him to be a prophet. He considers his life to be epic, and he thinks he carries a message of such importance that few in the church can understand him and even fewer appreciate him. He refuses to join a church, or any body of believers, because none of them give him his just due.

Instead of joining, he gathers followers who will sit under his teaching. But follower after follower eventually leaves his fold, or is asked to leave when they gently question anything the prophet says.

What are we to do?

We need to remember the call to prophetic humility: God's voice came to Balaam through the prophet's donkey. God doesn't call pastors, apostles, or prophets to confirm their greatness. Rather, the opposite: "He raises the poor from the dust and lifts the needy from the ash heap" (Ps. 113:7). God can make the littlest of us great, but he can't use the greatest among us until we become little.

If you are being used greatly for God, it says very little about you and very much about him.

There is a deep human longing for a life of significance. But we will only find our significance from God's love and *never* from a title or a service. We need to foster an inner vigilance against gaining an epic life from *any* God-given service or gifting.

A sure sign that we are looking to our gifting rather than to God is our treatment of fellow believers. If we refuse to join other believers, insisting instead that they join us, then we are in grave danger of misguided prophetic self-importance.

Confusing Desires with "Words"

Over the course of eight months, three different women told a college friend of mine that God said he should marry her. Assuming that God does not promote polygamy—a reasonable reading of Scripture—then at least two of these women didn't hear God.

I suspect that the "words" they heard were corrupted by the fact that my friend was six-foot-three, the captain of his high school football team, an honors student in engineering, and had a gentle disposition and wavy blond hair.

What are we to do?

True words from God will resonate deep within our hearts, even when they are exactly the opposite of what we want to hear. But deep longings also reverberate within us. We crave recognition, comfort, love, and a sense of significance—things no human on earth can fully or consistently satisfy.

So when a sense from God precisely parallels such a longing, we need extra caution and self-examination, because our desires can hinder our ability to discern. Is it really God speaking or just ourselves attempting to spiritualize a purely personal want? These are the times when we most need the safety of unbiased counsel from wise friends.

For the record, I have yet to hear of an attractive, successful man or woman who told a geeky, overweight, socially awkward, academically challenged acquaintance, "God said we are to get married."

Using "Words" to Get Our Way

A friend of mine served on a church leadership board when one of the church members, touched by a book he had read, asked if he could conduct a Sunday school class on that book. Although the book was outside the church's vision for that year, the board wanted to be open to God's agendas outside of their own, so they approved the class.

The following week, the member approached the board asking if the book's author could conduct an all-weekend retreat preceded by a four-week sermon series on the topic. When the board hesitated, the member added, "God told me this is what we are to do, and if you refuse, you are disobeying God."

Too often, "words" of God are used as battering rams to win arguments or to get our way.

What are we to do?

If we sense a word from God, let's hold on to it with humility. No matter how strongly we feel about what we've received, we should never bludgeon others into submitting to it. If God is behind that word, he will confirm it. It's not our job to force it into being.

If you hear a word of direction for a person or organization, feel free to share it—but humbly. Don't coerce others into obeying it. Your hearing may be faulty (yes, admit your human fallibility), or your sense of timing may be wrong, or God may not have wanted you to share it. Maybe he gave you an insight so you could pray for it.

I suggest that churches announce their plans with equal humility. Too many leaders boldly proclaim, "God has given us this vision for our church!" It would be better to say, "After prayer and consultation, the church leaders and I feel God calling us in this direction. But our hope is in God, not in our plans. We are committing this vision to God and praying that he directs our paths, even if they lead us in ways we don't envision."

What do we do when someone claims to give us a command based on a personal word from God? Let's prayerfully consider the message and wait for God's confirmation. If God wants us to do something, he won't rely on just one feeble human being to inform us, and he won't hide his direction from us. He confirms his words with Scripture, counsel, other words, and circumstances.

Consider the gifting of the person. Does he or she have a track record of hearing God? Is that person a mature believer who is good at distinguishing between their personal wants and God's words?

With those guidelines in mind, let's not discourage people from hearing God. Eli was a longtime priest, yet he humbly listened to the boy Samuel. Our own attitude likewise ought to be one of humility, whether we're giving or receiving a word.

The Left-Brained/Right-Brained Fallacy

I once heard a Christian speaker say, "Hearing God is a totally right-brained activity. We need to turn off our analytical thinking and lean into our intuition."

Perhaps it's a reaction to the Enlightenment's crowning of reason as king, but many Christians today feel that God's word only comes to us when we turn off our minds. They say we need to refrain from left-brain activity and fully lean into the creative, intuitive, spontaneous right brain.

One Christian leader even told me that "thinking is the Devil's territory."

What are we to do?

Let's not base the beauty of hearing God on the popularization of an outdated and unscientific theory. The right-brain/left-brain idea came from the work of Roger Sperry, who studied a specific set of brain surgery patients. Sperry himself claimed the idea had no broader value beyond those patients.

Numerous studies disprove the modern myth of right-brain/left-brain dominance.[1] Research shows that the analytical (left-brained) person actually analyzes better when *also* using the right brain, and the creative (right-brained) artist actually creates better when *also* using the left brain.

The Enlightenment may have divorced itself from the heart, but our feeling-oriented culture today wants to chop off the head. Both approaches undermine our ability to function. Dismissing the heart doesn't help us think better, and a spiritual lobotomy doesn't help us hear God better. God means us to be whole people, neither a heart-deprived Tin Man nor a lobotomized tomato.

God means us to be whole-brained. Rejection of the right or left brain is a rejection of God's plan for our whole being. When we listen for God's voice, we need to be open to the spontaneous thoughts God speaks to our minds, but we also need to exercise our reason, remembering the truths God speaks through Scripture, so we can distinguish between the voice of God and the voices of the world, our flesh, and the Devil.

Besides, if we can be deceived by bad thinking, we can also be deceived by bad spontaneous, intuitive perceptions. We need our whole, balanced selves.

Disingenuous Descriptions of Godly Dialogues

Too often—*far* too often—well-meaning people describe their conversations with God in unhelpful, misleading manners. They narrate their conversations with God as though they are dialogues written by playwrights:

God said: "Why are you so upset?"
I said: "I'm mad at my wife who yelled at me."
God said: "But you failed to take the trash out three weeks in a row."
I said: "Yes, but I've been really busy. And I hate taking out the trash."
God said: "You need to repent to your wife."
I said: "Yeah, I guess so. I really have been neglecting her too much."

What's wrong with this narrative description? Nothing at all if it represents what actually happened. But mostly it misrepresents how communication with God actually unfolds. The common result is discouragement when we ourselves don't experience that same kind of chummy banter with the God of creation. *What's wrong with us*, we wonder. "What's wrong" is rather the conversation model we've been handed.

What are we to do?

I used to find these dialogue descriptions intimidating and discouraging. My parents taught me to converse with God, but I've never had a running discussion with God feel like an Oscar Wilde dialogue. Never.

My frustration finally bore fruit. After hearing a speaker yet again tell of similar discourses, I finally got up the guts to talk with him in private. I asked him to explain how his conversation with God really went. He admitted that his dialogues with God were never as simple as he articulated. Rather, they were akin to my brainstorming with God: the speaker thought about an issue and invited God into that deliberation.

During his talks, he would recount those times of brainstorming prayer in dialogue form. It was simply a device for telling the story quickly. But in reality, a story he might teach as six dialogue interchanges might have taken hours of prayerful brainstorming.

I felt relieved but a little disgruntled.

Any time we tell a story of hearing God, we must use caution lest our storytelling discourage others. If we tell it in a fairy-tale fashion, others will believe that they've *never* heard God; yet all the while they may hear God more often and more clearly than we do. The only difference between them and us is honesty: they don't exaggerate or embroider their dialogues as we do.

The gift of hearing God is so precious and yet so untaught that we speakers and storytellers must use extra vigilance in recounting such encounters. If you really had a word-for-word dialogue with God as shown above, go ahead and share it, but let people know it's unusual.

If you are not the one person in three billion who hears God in back-and-forth dialogue, but instead are like the rest of the human race, then express the story as it occurred:

> I was concerned about a disagreement with my wife. I couldn't shake the anger, so I took some time to pray about it. While praying, I had a wide variety of thoughts—some good and from God, and probably some just from my flesh. In the end I realized that God was calling me to repent to my wife for neglect.

That is how the story happened, so just tell it like it was. No embellishment and no embroidery. If the way things actually happened was good enough to move you to repentance, then it will be good enough for the rest of us as well.

What About *Jesus Calling*, by Sarah Young? Is It Also Excessive or Questionable?

In 2004, Sarah Young published a sleeper titled *Jesus Calling: Enjoying Peace in His Presence*. After four years of modest sales, like a tactical nuke, the book exploded onto the Christian devotional scene with sales of over ten million copies. In it, Young shares words she believes she heard from God while meditating on Scripture.

While Young's book enjoys wildly successful sales, many Christian leaders express significant cautions: concerns over her first-person prose in the name of God, questions regarding its oversimplified focus on peace, and fears that readers find more spiritual life in her book than they do in Scripture.

What are we to do?

First, I applaud Sarah Young's example of hearing God through scriptural meditation. That's the point of chapters 5, 6, and 10 in this book: "Hearing God in Meditation," "Speaking to Listen," and "Questions: Connecting with God." Sarah's daily devotionals always include the Scripture passages that inspired her thoughts. She reads these passages as living words, just as real for her as they were for the original writers. Then, through prayer and reflection, she writes blended paraphrases. In that way, her book is a great model.

Her first-person prose simply requires heightened vigilance on our part: we absolutely need to remember that her words are a fallible human's sense of God speaking. Sarah herself warns us that "these writings were not inspired as Scripture" and that "the Bible is, of course, the only inerrant Word of God."[2] I find that many readers forget her preface and read the book's first-person prose as though it is the equivalent of oracles of God—which, as Sarah insists, it is not.

Sarah Young battles with a debilitating infection, Lyme disease, and the peace she senses may be God's battlefield dressings in her struggle with pain. Perhaps her words resonate with us, but if she is hearing from God, she is hearing God's words *for her*, not necessarily God's words *for us*. Let's use our spiritual, Scripture-formed minds to distinguish between God's life-changing words and the tickling that our itching ears want to hear.

Peace is indeed a major theme in Scripture, but it is not the only theme. When we review all of Scripture, we see a complex, multi-themed, transcendent God. His ways are not our ways, and what we *think* we need is not always what God *knows* we need. We think we need peace in this moment, but God might think we need surgery.

If we discover ourselves finding more life in Sarah Young's words than in Scripture, let's not disparage her. Rather, let's examine ourselves. It's always more life-giving to hear from God ourselves than to overhear God speaking to another person. Let's not be like the Israelites who said to Moses, "You speak [with] us, . . . but do not let God speak [with] us" (Exod. 20:19).

We can learn to hear God speaking to us in the Bible by meditation, by speaking to listen (paraphrasing), and by connecting with him through answering his questions in Scripture.

If we journal, then let's use caution in our own use of the first person. My personal approach is to avoid unequivocal statements like, "Sam, attend that retreat." Instead, I write, "I *thought* I heard God tell me to attend that retreat." It's a nuance, but it leaves room for humility—and we absolutely must approach any word we hear with the meekness appropriate to imperfect people.

(Note: My third-person suggestion is merely my own method for approaching first-person writing with care. Some people I know journal in the first person with no problem, because they always keep in mind their human frailty and capacity for error.)

The chapter on "Brainstorming with God" is my personal version of journaling. We invite God into our thinking about *everything*, from handling finances to examining hurts and anger—but we also (a) use spiritual reason to block out uninvited voices, (b) prayerfully reflect on all that we hear to discern if it is the voice of God or indigestion, and (c) hold on to all these "words" with a spirit of humility, knowing they don't have the certainty of Scripture.

Guidance Through Wisdom

Our lives overflow with moments of decision: what to study in college, whom to marry, whether to accept a new job offer, and how much TV to allow our kids to watch. We look for decision-making tools. Even believers who reject God's extrabiblical voice today will agree that he still guides us.

Many argue that God limits his guidance to wisdom and his Word. His Word will tell us not to steal money or oppress our employees, but it doesn't tell us whether to be a plumber, teacher, or engineer. When Scripture doesn't speak to a specific situation, some teach that the only remaining God-given guidance tools are reason and wisdom.

What are we to do?

The vast majority of decisions are made on the basis of wisdom shaped by the Word. We daily make hundreds of decisions: which route to take to work, what to cook for dinner, which shoes to wear, and how many cups of coffee to drink. Of our countless decisions, I would guess that 99.99 percent are made with wisdom. At least, we hope it's wisdom.

Hopefully some of our decisions also come from the Word. While Scripture doesn't tell us how to coordinate our clothes or which job offer to accept, it does teach us to care for our bodies and to examine our motives. Maybe we want that new job because of its increased salary even though it means we'll spend less time at home.

"Deism" is the heresy that believes God created the earth with moral, spiritual, and physical laws; then he set it spinning around the sun and sat back to watch it as though in a movie theater—with no more interaction, contact, or communication. The "wisdom and the Word alone" teaching implies a kind of *biblical deism*, as though God has done his bit—given his Word and our reason—and now he is a mere spectator, watching the movie of our lives to see if we do our bit.

There is thus an implication that only the brightest people with the highest IQ can really get God's guidance.

The depth of my relationship with my kids increases as they grow older. They are adults and are making great decisions. I love it when they call me for advice, not so I can instruct them but so we can talk. I don't say, "I've taught you all I have to offer." I say, "Thanks for calling. Let's talk about that new job offer. What about it do you like and what about it gives you concern?"

Can we think of any possible reason in the world—based on wisdom *and* God's Word—that God wouldn't want to converse with us the same way? God is a far better Father than I'll ever be.

Guidance and Finding God's Perfect Plan

Another Christian guidance school teaches the *blueprint theory*. This model tells us that God has a plan—a blueprint, if you will—of every step of our lives. Every single choice we encounter has a right and a wrong answer, and every decision we make will keep us on God's path or place us on ungodly detours.

The blueprint theory teaches that we discover God's plan with two tools: paying attention to God-given signs and examining the open or shut doors God places in our paths. If there is a blueprint for our lives, God must guide us in the minutest choices of everyday life. There is one, and only one, perfect plan for our lives, and we miss that plan at our peril.[3]

What are we to do?

God *will* offer signs and he *will* open and shut doors, but his guidance is not limited. In fact, God himself often asks us to persist along a path even though every door seems shut and guiding signs seem absent. The boy David was called to be king, and for a time every door opened, as in his fight with Goliath and his appointment as a captain of Israel's army. But then for a time even city gates slammed in his face.

God's call to persistence means that there are times when we are directed outside of open doors, because all the doors seem shut. Some other guidance is provided, and it is that direction we are to follow. Even when every possible door seems slammed in our faces.

The biggest problem with the blueprint theory is its lack of human involvement in a connection with God. When God gave Adam and Eve the garden of Eden, he put them in charge. He didn't direct where to plant the orange trees and how to lay out paths. He gave the couple creative authority. When God walked with them in the cool of the day, it wasn't to give them a blueprint for the rosebushes; it was to talk, for them to have a conversational relationship with the ultimate Creator. God wasn't opening and closing garden gates.

If we follow the blueprint teaching to its logical conclusion, it means we need precise, unmistakable guidance on every decision we ever make, from the cola brand we drink to the spouse we marry. *After all, we want to be in accord with God's perfect plan, right?* But what if his "will" was a different career than we chose? Will we forever be out of his will? Are we condemned to Plan B for the rest of our lives?

God forms godly desires in our hearts. A huge component of God's guidance for our lives is our discovery of those godly desires, accompanied by the death of our fleshly desires. In other words, much of God's guidance is found in the discovery of whom he designed us to be. God delights to see us grow up into mature men and women of his design as we are led by the deepest desires he places within us.

Godly guidance comes to us primarily out of a daily walk with him; it is the conversation that he wants more than our impersonal interpretation of signs and doors. He even leaves room for error—in fact, his orchestration can turn our worst screwups into gold. Because God's idea of perfection is different from ours and far more merciful. It's about relationship and grace, not reading every sign just right.

Yoga, Transcendental Meditation, and Eastern Religious Practices

Maybe it was the Beatles who popularized Eastern religions. Maybe it was just our Western culture's rejection of Enlightenment's rationalism. Whatever led us to this point, we are now bombarded with mystical, irrational, mind-emptying spirituality. Anything Christian is out of date. Everything Eastern is perfectly acceptable.

I recently enrolled in a weight loss clinic, and the dietician—the *dietician!*—gave an hour-long lecture on the value of meditation for weight loss. And she didn't mean Christian meditation. She began with Buddhist breathing concentration and proceeded to "mindfulness" teachings, the use of gongs, and finding our "inner balance."

She unabashedly referenced Buddhist and Brahman spirituality as she coached yoga exercises. In the spirit of inclusivity, she claimed we can practice all yoga exercises no matter what our religion. She is one of scores of yoga advocates I know. Many of my Christian friends teach either a secularized or a "Christianized" form of yoga.

What are we to do?

The first commandment says, "You shall have no other gods before me" (Exod. 20:3). But the word *before* means more than "precedence"; it mostly means "presence." It's not merely suggesting, "Let no other god take priority over me"; it commands us, "Bring no other gods into my presence." And his "presence" means every part of our reborn lives.

Throughout the Old Testament, God continually admonishes his people to put away idols; to shun even a hint of other gods; and even at the risk of their lives, to avoid mixing the local gods with the religion of the Bible. Yet Solomon, wise as he was, was also a master at syncretism.

Mixing pagan practices with true worship of God was the root of Solomon's horrific, devastating, spiritual demise.

We modern believers rarely think of idols. Whom do you know who has a hidden shrine to Baal in their garden? Our idols are subtler and a bit more insidious: the gods of the perfect family, or good looks, or people-pleasing. These idols are harder to root out.

The only obvious religious syncretism of our times is our mixture of Eastern religious practices with Christianity. It's the Christian who practices yoga for fitness or Eastern meditation for relaxation.

At first blush, it appears harmless: you've taken out the Buddhist mantras. But these practices arise from religions that do not worship the God of the Bible. Somewhere between us and the Buddhist monk in our training ancestry, someone decided yoga was safe as long as "X" was removed. Do we know who that removal expert was? Do we know their spiritual maturity? Do we know if the removed "X" was enough? If *you* were that removal expert, do you really trust yourself enough to know what good you can learn from a religion that is contrary to the Bible?

Solomon, in all his wisdom, was deceived. Do we claim superior wisdom to Solomon?

Idols appealed to the Israelites. Why was that? Wasn't God all that they needed? Yes, he was, but they wanted faster or different results. They turned to other gods for crops, fertility, and peace of mind. We do the same thing with yoga and Transcendental Meditation. Idols promise one thing, and for a time it feels like they deliver, but their end is hell on earth. At the very least.

Jesus offers meditation teaching too: "Consider the lilies, how they grow: they neither toil nor spin, yet I tell you, even Solomon in all his glory was not arrayed like one of these" (Luke 12:27). The word *consider* is a meditation word. It means to think deeply about this truth. Eastern religions empty the mind in order to block out the world. Jesus invites us to fill the mind with his words and creation. Both practices result in a type of peace, but only one kind of peace is from God.

My critique of yoga will be unpopular with some readers. Many who disagree with me use yoga workouts as an opportunity for Scripture meditation as described in chapters 5, 6, and 10. They may claim this as an area of Christian liberty (Rom. 14:12–16). While I do not wish to offend further, let me urge such practitioners to consider the story of Daniel, Shadrach, Meshach, and Abednego (Dan. 1:5–20). These four young men refused to "defile" themselves with any health practice that conflicted with God's Word, and their refusal seemed senseless to the culture around them. Yet their faithfulness to God resulted in noticeably greater fitness than all who listened to the health experts of their time, and they found favor with God and man.

God's ways are mysterious. Sometimes his commands simply don't make sense. That's why God urges us to have "faith *in* him" rather than asking us to "agree *with* him." Oftentimes it is only after we have walked in noncomprehending faith that Scripture promises to make clear the things that puzzle us today (John 13:7).

Notes

Preface: My Parents' Gift of Extraordinary Ordinariness
1. Mark Galli, "The Top 50 Books That Have Shaped Evangelicals," *Christianity Today*, October 6, 2006.
2. Rosalind Rinker, *Prayer: Conversing with God* (Grand Rapids: Zondervan, 1959), 23.
3. Robert Watson Frazer, *A Literary History of India* (London, 1898), 144.
4. John 19:30.
5. Lewis says he found this poem in an old notebook with no author's name attached. I speculate that Lewis himself wrote it. Excerpt from *Letters to Malcom: Chiefly on Prayer* by C. S. Lewis. Copyright © 1964, 1963 by C. S. Lewis PTE Ltd. and renewed 1992, 1991 by Arthur Owen Barfield. Reprinted by permission of Houghton Mifflin Harcourt Publishing Company. All rights reserved.

Chapter 1: The First Time I Heard God's Voice
1. Excerpt from *Letters to Malcom: Chiefly on Prayer* by C. S. Lewis. Copyright © 1964, 1963 by C. S. Lewis PTE Ltd. and renewed 1992, 1991 by Arthur Owen Barfield. Reprinted by permission of Houghton Mifflin Harcourt Publishing Company. All rights reserved.

Chapter 2: Conversation Is the Point
1. Bob Hartig, my editor, in an email to me dated March 20, 2015. Used by permission.

2. John Donne, "Holy Sonnet 14," from *Holy Sonnets,* in *John Donne: The Major Works; Including Songs and Sonnets and Sermons,* ed. John Carey (London: Oxford University Press, 1990), 178.

Chapter 3: How to Recognize the Voice of God

1. Charles Stanley, *How to Listen to God* (Nashville: Nelson, 1985), 73–74.
2. Commonly but unverifiably attributed to the German-born American physician Martin H. Fischer.
3. Oswald Chambers, *My Utmost for His Highest: An Updated Edition in Today's Language,* ed. James Reimann (Grand Rapids: Discovery House, 1992), August 13.
4. E. Stanley Jones, *A Song of Ascents: A Spiritual Autobiography* (Nashville: Abingdon, 1990), 190.
5. Philip Yancey, as quoted by Priscilla Shirer in *Discerning the Voice of God: How to Recognize When God Speaks* (Chicago: Moody Publishers, 2007), 54.
6. Dallas Willard, *Hearing God: Developing a Conversational Relationship with God* (Downers Grove, IL: InterVarsity, 2012), 135. Emphasis in original.
7. William Guthrie, *The Christian's Great Interest* (Glasgow, 1828), 156.
8. Peter Lord, *Hearing God: An Easy-to-Follow, Step-by-Step Guide to Two-Way Communication with God* (Bloomington, MN: Chosen Books, 2011), 45.

Chapter 4: What Are the Scriptures For?

1. This quote has repeatedly been attributed to C. S. Lewis, and I love it, but I am unable to track down its original source. It is attributed to Lewis by David Sitton, *Reckless Abandon* (Greenville, SC: Ambassador International, 2013) and by Larry Tomczak, *Reckless Abandon: The Call to Be a Spiritual Pioneer* (Lake Mary, FL: Charisma House, 2002), 88.
2. Romans 8:28.
3. John Calvin, *Institutes of the Christian Religion,* ed. John T. McNeill (Louisville: Westminster, 1960), 3.2.36, 583.

4. C. S. Lewis, "Learning in War-Time," *The Weight of Glory: And Other Addresses* (New York: HarperCollins, 1980), 57.

5. Nicolas Wolterstorff, *Lament for a Son* (Grand Rapids: Eerdmans, 1987), 90.

Chapter 5: Hearing God in Meditation

1. Quoted in Richard Foster, *Celebration of Discipline: The Path to Spiritual Growth* (New York: HarperCollins, 1998), 19.

2. Jordan Aumann, "Spiritual Theology," accessed April 4, 2016, https://archive.org/stream/SpiritualTheologyByFr.JordanAu mannO.p/AumannO.p.SpiritualTheologyall_djvu.txt.

3. Søren Kierkegaard, *The Soul of Kierkegaard: Selections from His Journals*, ed. Alexander Dru (Mineola, NY: Dover Publications, 2003), 117.

4. Timothy Keller, *Prayer: Experiencing Awe and Intimacy with God* (New York: Penguin, 2014), 149. The questions he's referring to here are (1) What did the original author intend to convey to his readers? and (2) How does this passage relate to the Bible as a whole, the gospel message, and the main narrative arc of the Bible?

5. Edmund P. Clowney, *CM: Christian Meditation* (Vancouver: Regent College Publishing, 2002), 12.

6. Ibid., 13.

7. Keller, *Prayer,* 179.

Chapter 6: Speaking to Listen

1. William Strunk Jr. and E. B. White, *The Elements of Style* (New York: Macmillan Publishing Co., Inc., 1979), Introduction, xvi.

2. Augustine of Hippo, *On the Trinity*, Book XV, Chapter 10.

3. For example, Jesus quotes Psalm 82:6 when he says, "Is it not written in your Law, 'I said, you are gods'?" (John 10:34). Jesus calls it "the law" when he quotes the Psalms.

4. C. S. Lewis, *God in the Dock: Essays on Theology and Ethics* (Grand Rapids: Eerdmans, 1970), 98.

5. This quote is popularly attributed to Albert Einstein. Many,

however, dispute Einstein's authorship, and they attribute it (or variants of it) to other physicists. I find the phrase delightfully wise, and I hope someday that my own grandmothers will introduce me to its truly creative, original author.

6. *The Message* is an example of an entire Bible paraphrased (and translated) by a man of devotion, Eugene Peterson. His insights into God's Word have inspired and challenged millions, all because he wanted to speak God's own words back to God.

7. This quote is also often attributed to Einstein. Its most likely origin, however, is a paraphrase of an Einstein speech, "On the Method of Theoretical Physics," delivered in the Herbert Spencer Lecture (Oxford, June 10, 1933), and the earliest printed paraphrase was by Roger Sessions in the *New York Times* (January 8, 1950).

8. C. S. Lewis, "Learning in War-Time," *The Weight of Glory: And Other Addresses* (New York: HarperCollins, 1980), 52.

9. J. I. Packer, *Knowing God* (Downers Grove, IL: InterVarsity, 1993), 16.

10. C. S. Lewis, *Reflections on the Psalms* (New York: First Mariner Books, 2012), 95.

11. C. S. Lewis, *Reflections on the Psalms* (New York: Houghton Mifflin Harcourt, 2012), 94.

Chapter 9: Hijacking the Conversation

1. St. Bonaventure, *The Life of St. Francis*, trans. Ewert Cousins (New York: HarperCollins, 2005), 14.

2. Elisabeth Elliot, *Through Gates of Splendor* (Carol Stream, IL: Tyndale House, 1996), 267.

3. C. S. Lewis, *God in the Dock: Essays on Theology and Ethics* (Grand Rapids: Eerdmans, 1970), 88–89.

4. The book's real subtitle is slightly different, but when I read it I personalized it; it seemed almost a direct word from God to me. The actual title and subtitle are, *Sacred Marriage: What If God Designed Marriage to Make Us Holy More Than to Make Us Happy*, by Gary L. Thomas (Grand Rapids: Zondervan, 2000).

Chapter 11: Cultivating A Holy Curiosity

1. Albert Einstein, "Old Man's Advice to Youth," *Life*, May 2, 1955, 65.
2. Ian Leslie, *Curious: The Desire to Know and Why Your Future Depends on It* (New York: Basic Books, 2014), xviii.
3. John Carmody, *Reexamining Conscience* (New York: Seabury, 1982), 18.
4. C. S. Lewis, *The Screwtape Letters* (New York: HarperCollins, 1996), 43.
5. Oswald Chambers, *My Utmost for His Highest: An Updated Edition in Today's Language*, ed. James Reimann (Grand Rapids: Discovery House, 1992), January 30.

Chapter 12: "How Can I Know It's God's Voice?"

1. I read the article more than twenty years ago. I no longer remember where I read it, but the insight has stuck with me. The quote is my paraphrase of the unknown author's conclusion.
2. Oswald Chambers, *My Utmost for His Highest: An Updated Edition in Today's Language*, ed. James Reimann (Grand Rapids: Discovery House, 1992), August 28.
3. E. Stanley Jones, *A Song of Ascents: A Spiritual Autobiography* (Nashville: Abingdon, 1990), 190.

Chapter 13: Friendship with the Real God

1. Oswald Chambers, *My Utmost for His Highest: An Updated Edition in Today's Language*, ed. James Reimann (Grand Rapids: Discovery House, 1992), February 7.
2. Rosalind Rinker, *Prayer: Conversing with God* (Grand Rapids: Zondervan, 1959), 23.
3. A. W. Tozer, *The Knowledge of the Holy: The Attributes of God: Their Meaning in Christian Life* (New York: HarperCollins, 1961), 1.
4. W. H. Auden, *Prose: The Complete Works of Auden*, vol. 2, *1939–1948*, ed. Edward Mendelson (Princeton: Princeton University Press, 2002), 196.
5. C. S. Lewis, "Is Theology Poetry?" in *The Weight of Glory: And Other Addresses* (New York: HarperCollins, 1980), 139.

6. Ibid., 38.
7. C. S. Lewis, *God in the Dock: Essays on Theology and Ethics* (Grand Rapids: Eerdmans, 1970), 166.
8. Auden, *Prose*, vol. 2, 196.
9. I reverse the order of a great phrase first coined by American humorist Finley Dunne over a hundred years ago as he mocked the hypocrisy and self-importance of the press. His original words were, "comforts th' afflicted, afflicts th' comfortable." Finley Peter Dunne, *Observations by Mr. Dooley* (New York: Harper & Brothers, 1906), 240.
10. Norman Grubb, *Touching the Invisible* (Fort Washington, PA: Christian Literature Crusade, 1940), 22.
11. Hudson Taylor, as quoted by Dr. and Mrs. Howard Taylor, *Hudson Taylor's Spiritual Secret* (Chicago: Moody Publishers, 2009), 180.

Chapter 14: Emotions and Experiences of God
1. Pascal's note, known as the "Memorial," is widely available on the Internet. For a great treatment of it, see chapter 5, "The Night of Fire," in Marvin Richard O'Connell, *Blaise Pascal: Reasons of the Heart* (Grand Rapids: Eerdmans, 1997).
2. William R. Moody, *The Life of Dwight L. Moody* (Albany, OR: Book for the Ages, 1997), 127.

Chapter 15: God Speaks in Our Detours
1. Churchill's actual words were, "I felt as if I were walking with destiny, and that all my past life had been but a preparation for this hour and for this trial." From "Churchill and the Great Republic: The Finest Hour," Library of Congress, http://www.loc.gov/exhibits/churchill/wc-hour.html.
2. C. S. Lewis, *The Problem of Pain* (New York: HarperCollins, 2009), 91.
3. Thomas à Kempis, *The Imitation of Christ*, bk. 4, *On the Blessed Sacrament*, ch. 20.
4. G. Campbell Morgan, *The True Estimate of Life and How to Live* (Chicago: Moody Publishers, n.d.), 76.

Chapter 16: Hearing God in the Ordinary

1. Oswald Chambers, *My Utmost for His Highest: An Updated Edition in Today's Language*, ed. James Reimann (Grand Rapids: Discovery House, 1992), February 7.
2. Ibid., February 13.
3. James Dobson, "The Will of God," *Focus on the Family*, broadcast December 3, 1982.

Chapter 17: God Shouts in His Silence

1. Nicholas Wolterstorff, *Lament for a Son* (Grand Rapids: Eerdmans, 1987), 90.
2. Oswald Chambers, *My Utmost for His Highest: An Updated Edition in Today's Language*, ed. James Reimann (Grand Rapids: Discovery House, 1992), January 3.
3. Ibid., January 12.
4. C. S. Lewis, *Letters to Malcolm: Chiefly on Prayer* (Orlando: Harcourt, 1992), 44.
5. John R. W. Stott, *The Cross of Christ* (Downers Grove, IL: InterVarsity, 1986), 160.
6. Elisabeth Elliot. This story was first given as a talk to the Inter-Varsity Student Mission Convention, Urbana, IL, December 1976. It was later published as a small pamphlet titled *The Glory of God's Will* (Lincoln, NE: Gateway to Joy, 1982), 3–4.

Chapter 18: The God Who Guides

1. Oswald Chambers, *My Utmost for His Highest: An Updated Edition in Today's Language*, ed. James Reimann (Grand Rapids: Discovery House, 1992), November 14.
2. Edmund P. Clowney, "The Glory of the Coming Lord: Discovering Christ in the Old Testament," *Modern Reformation* 4, no. 6, Nov./Dec. 1995.
3. Frederick Buechner, *Now and Then: A Memoir of Vocation* (New York: HarperCollins, 1991), 87.

Appendix A: Answers to the Arguments
1. Dallas Willard, *Hearing God: Developing a Conversational Relationship with God* (Downers Grove, IL: InterVarsity, 2012), 136–37. Emphasis in original.
2. E. Stanley Jones, *A Song of Ascents: A Spiritual Autobiography* (Nashville: Abingdon, 1990), 191.
3. Willard, *Hearing God*, 137. Emphasis in original.
4. Gordon T. Smith, *Listening to God in Times of Choice: The Art of Discerning God's Will* (Downers Grove, IL: InterVarsity, 1997), 36.
5. Willard, *Hearing God*, 142–43. Emphasis in original.

Appendix B: Questionable and Excessive Practices
1. See these articles: "Right Brain, Left Brain? Scientists Debunk Popular Theory," *Huffington Post*, updated August 20, 2013, http://www.huffingtonpost.com/2013/08/19/right-brain-left-brain-debunked_n_3762322.html; "Why the Left-Brain Right-Brain Myth Will Probably Never Die," https://www.psychologytoday.com/blog/brain-myths/201206/why-the-left-brain-right-brain-myth-will-probably-never-die; "Despite what you've been told, you aren't 'left-brained' or 'right-brained,'" http://www.theguardian.com/commentisfree/2013/nov/16/left-right-brain-distinction-myth; "Left Brain vs. Right: It's a Myth, Research Finds," http://www.livescience.com/39373-left-brain-right-brain-myth.html.
2. Sarah Young, *Jesus Calling: Enjoying Peace in His Presence* (Nashville: Nelson, 2004), xiii–xiv.
3. Gordon T. Smith provides an excellent analysis of this guidance method in chapter 1, "Dancing with God," in Smith, *Listening to God in Times of Choice: The Art of Discerning God's Will* (Downers Grove, IL: InterVarsity, 1997).